D1499610

FASHION SHOWMANSHIP

FASHION SHOWMANSHIP

Everything You Need To Know
To Give A Fashion
Show

KAY CORINTH

JOHN WILEY
& SONS, INC.

New York / London
Sydney / Toronto

This book is lovingly dedicated to three distinguished women who have helped make American fashion great . . . and with whom I have had the happy privilege and honor of working:

To Julia Coburn Antolini,
innovator and leader in fashion education

To Enid Annenberg Haupt,
editor-in-chief of *Seventeen* Magazine and creator of good fashion for young women

To the memory of the late Tobé Coller Davis,
noted fashion and merchandising authority and the first American stylist

Contents

1

Show Business in the Fashion World

Whenever you are involved in any way with a fashion show, you are involved in show business. The fashion show may be a live production with the excitement of a Broadway first night, or a movie with the glamour of Hollywood, or a television feature with the scope of reaching thousands or even millions of viewers. Although the fashions are the stars, attractive models are called on to present them, often backed by celebrities, actors, or dancers. Joining the action to provide the showmanship are fashion authorities, designers, producers, directors, musicians, and many other specialists along with their staffs.

Traditionally a "fashion show" means the presentation of wearing apparel, accessories, and beauty trends in some type of show format before an audience. While it may possibly be a still show with clothes exhibited on inanimate mannequins, or even on headless dressmaker forms, the term "fashion show" has come to imply the showing of clothes on live models. It also implies some kind of staging for the purpose of dramatizing the merchandise and entertaining the audience.

FASHION MAKES A PRESTIGIOUS SHOW

Because the introduction and wearing of new fashions traditionally have been associated with the wealthy or celebrated, the fashion show has always typified a prestigious presentation of fashion. In countries where a monarchy still exists, members of royal families are frequent attendants at fashion shows. In England, models must be able to curtsy if Princess Margaret or the Queen Mother happens to be present. On these occasions, protocol demands that the model walk straight up to the royal personage and make a curtsy before proceeding to show her garment.

The attendance of the Duke and Duchess of Windsor at one show threw the cast into a frenzy—they were not sure whether to curtsy before the Duchess and recognize her as royalty. The girls did decide to make the curtsy, thereby giving royal status to the Duchess, at least during the show.

Mrs. Lyndon B. Johnson awarded the highest recognition to fashion and the fashion show in the United States when she planned and sponsored "How to Discover America in Style" in the State Dining Room of the White House on February 29, 1968. This was the first fashion show ever held in the White House. It was given as entertainment for the wives of governors attending a conference in Washington. It also tied in with the President's campaign to promote travel within the United States and Mrs. Johnson's national beautification program.

Surely American fashion reached its pinnacle when models were fitted in Lincoln's Bedroom, made their changes during the show in the East Room, and marched down a specially constructed runway in the State Dining Room. Commentary was provided by Nancy White, editor-in-chief of *Harper's Bazaar*.

The first fashion show ever held in the White House in Washington, 1968. Designer Rudi Gernreich, center, watches one of his own designs being modeled.

THE FASHION SHOW MEANS BUSINESS

Although a fashion show must be entertaining to be successful, it is actually given for business reasons. Each sponsor of a show has a particular goal in mind. Usually it is simply to sell fashion merchandise. But it may have public relations as its primary aim and selling as a secondary result. Even though many kinds of organizations produce fashion shows as pure entertainment or as a benefit to raise money for a charitable, civic, or educational cause, some company provides the clothes for public relations and sales reasons.

The power of fashion is such a strong force in the selling of merchandise that other industries, businesses, and services have adopted the fashion show as a means of promoting their products. The particular product—whether a new car or a new soft drink—may be linked in some way to fashion apparel and presented in a fashion show. These are called "industrial shows."

Fashion shows have thus developed into a successful medium for promoting and selling not only apparel but also many other kinds of products. They take place somewhere every day including Sundays. There is scarcely a village or hamlet that doesn't enjoy its version of a fashion show for some purpose.

WHY FASHION MAKES A GOOD SHOW

Psychologists, sociologists, writers, and others have theorized about why the human being wears clothes and otherwise adorns his body. For the purpose of fashion, the reason is not important. There are undoubtedly many explanations. Females and males of all ages like to wear and enjoy clothes that are in fashion; they like to use cosmetics, toiletries, and fragrances that are favored at the moment. Even hair styling is an important part of this fashion urge.

Most normal persons are eager to know what is new in fashion, but they want authority behind the fashion before they will buy and wear it themselves. They want to know that a new fashion is right and good, as well as how and where to wear it. There is no better authority for a new fashion than to have it modeled by a person who has flair and a feeling for wearing clothes. Add the drama of a show, and the impact is almost irresistible.

Women Like to See Clothes Modeled

Although women especially want to be individual in appearance, they still desire to dress within the framework of current fashion.

One of the most beautiful and original fashion shows ever given was staged to introduce Springmaid towels by designer Pucci. The entire presentation was in abstract dance choreographed by Alwin Nikolais and performed by his company to an electronic score. Courtesy of Springs Mills.

Shows sponsored by stores or shops that are fashion leaders, or that feature fashions by good designers, offer one of the best ways to keep up with what is coming into fashion, including new ideas in accessories, beauty, and hair styling.

Since the majority of women, of course, are not fashion professionals, they lack self-confidence in selecting and buying clothes. This is especially true of teen-age girls who are just beginning to buy their own clothes and develop a personality. Any female likes to see how another

The bath towel becomes a work of art in the Springmaid showing at the George Abbott Theatre in New York. Here, towel patterns are projected on the abstract dancers who wear sack-like costumes. Courtesy of Springs Mills.

The weaving of towels provides a theme for the Alwin Nikolais dancers in Springmaid's Broadway showing of towel fashions. Courtesy of Springs Mills.

To dramatize fashions in bed and bath linens, Fieldcrest commissioned twenty-five designers to create a fashion collection from their merchandise. An evening ensemble by John Moore, made from a pink sheet and blanket, being modeled at the showing, "Lady, You're Putting Me On!"

woman or girl looks in an outfit, and how she has accessorized it. She especially likes to see a model outfitted in a new fashion because the model represents the paragon of appearance and glamour.

Seeing clothes on a hanger does not give the same impression as seeing them on a model. The hanger presents clothes in a flat, two-dimensional way, while the body is three-dimensional, rounded, and mobile. Of course, a woman may try on a garment in a store and see how she looks in it, but she has more confidence if she sees another woman wearing it. Also she may be inclined to pass up and never even try on something that might look well on her, but that lacks "hanger appeal."

The French couture has shown clothes on live mannequins from the beginning. Now the clothes in the collections are shown with accessories especially designed to complement them and compose a total fashion look. The American woman can rarely shop this way because there are only a handful of made-to-order houses in the United States, and these usually cater to a wealthy clientele. Her chance to see clothes modeled is the fashion show. Her immediate response after the show is evidence of the importance of showing clothes on a moving body. It is not uncommon for a woman or girl to buy a complete outfit with accessories exactly as it was modeled in a show. It is quite usual for a model, whether professional or amateur, to buy a total outfit that she has modeled herself. The store's assembling of the "look" on her gives her confidence.

The Male and the Fashion Show

Until the 1960s, most of the color and change in clothes for the past two centuries was confined to female apparel. Male clothing was drab in color and conservative in design. Furthermore, men were afraid to vary very far from the norm of conservatism for fear of being considered effeminate and foppish. There was rarely ever a men's fashion show, except trade shows for menswear buyers.

The Beatles and other young sound groups changed all this when they came on the scene in the early 1960s. As a part of the images they projected, they originated new and different styling, fabrics, and colors in their clothes, as well as new fashions in men's hair styling, thereby firing the first shot in the "peacock revolution."

Before this time, the inclusion of male models and male clothing in a fashion show was purely incidental as a foil for the women's clothing and models. When the big fashion change occurred and it became acceptable for a man to look individual too in a choice of new fashions, it was natural that the male fashion show, or a combination of female and male, should emerge because men now had the same need as women to see new fashions assembled and modeled. However, men's fashion shows are still rare (except for trade shows) and may never reach the popularity of women's shows.

THE PURELY PROFESSIONAL SHOW

The majority of fashion shows are given for consumers by retail stores or by organizations that borrow the clothes from a store. However, many shows are never seen by a consumer. These are the "trade" shows within the fashion industry, given by and for professionals.

Apparel and accessory manufacturers of all types present their seasonal lines or collections at "showings" or fashion shows attended by store buyers and merchandising executives. Associations of manufacturers frequently join together in a fashion show to promote the entire industry to buyers. The press may be invited to these trade shows, or a special press showing may be given.

Other industries also borrow fashion to enliven and glamorize their merchandise during their trade or press presentations. An example of this was the introduction to the press of Campbell Soup Company's canned puddings in a fashion-show format at the Plaza Hotel in New York. While impeccably uniformed waiters paraded through the room carrying various fancy concoctions made from the puddings, a magazine editor described the puddings in fashion terms.

A GOOD SHOW DEMANDS A "PRO"

In light of this tremendous popularity of fashion shows, almost everyone is likely to become involved at some time, in some way, in the production of a show. Lured by the prospect of fun and glamour that this little bit of show business offers, many neophytes blithely take on this responsibility without realizing the hard work and know-how required. Many professionals fail because of the lack of knowledge about some aspects of a show.

Giving a fashion show embraces many different areas and considerations. Beginners are unaware of all the small details that must be handled. Members of clubs and organizations frequently embark on a fashion show, believing that all that is necessary is to borrow clothes from a store or shop and have their members model them while someone describes each nip and tuck. Since the very name "fashion show" implies something more, this obviously is not enough to interest and hold the attention of an audience. A polished production demands the know-how of a "pro."

For the professional or the amateur, this book discusses every phase of planning and producing a successful fashion show. It also brings together, for the first time, the fascinating history of the show and modeling.

CALL IT A FASHION SHOW

The first step toward being a pro in fashion-show business is to use the correct terminology. The name for the presentation of any kind of merchandise that employs fashion is "fashion show." Many times it is incorrectly called a "style show." The terms *fashion* and *style* are distinguished in the following way.

Fashion. This word is correctly applied to the prevailing and accepted clothes, beauty, home furnishings, automobiles, houses, and even food. Fashion influences almost everything that relates to life, including even words and language.

Style. This term is a little more difficult to define. Webster calls style "a distinctive or characteristic manner." For example, there are styles in writing, in painting, and in acting. There are also styles in dressing. You might say, "She dresses in a conservative style," or "a luxurious style," or "a tailored style." Her clothes can express the newest fashions within any one of these styles. Style is a way of doing something.

One other word must be defined because it is frequently confused with fashion. This is *fad*, which is something that catches on quickly, becomes a craze or a rage for a short time, and then dies as fast as it appeared. The granny dress that swept across the country late in 1966 is an example of a fad. It was all over and forgotten within several months. A fad like this can sometimes make a fashion show very amusing because of its novelty and news value.

2

The History of Fashion Shows

Although the fashion show as it exists today is a twentieth-century innovation, almost 600 years ago women found a means of obtaining fashion information and seeing clothes worn and accessorized. This included hairdressing and the total look.

THE FASHION DOLLS

In 1391, Queen Isabella of Bavaria, wife of Charles VI of France, originated the idea of having a life-sized figure made and dressed in the latest court fashions as a gift for Queen Anne of Bohemia who was the wife of Richard II, the king of England. This may have been similar to present-day display mannequins, but it was called a "fashion doll." Apparently it was evident, even then, that fashion is best shown on a body—even the lifeless body of a doll.

Subsequent entries in court records reveal that the sending of dolls from one court to another became a custom and a compliment. These were called "model dolls," which may be the beginning of the use of the word "model" to designate someone who shows clothes.

The custom of circulating fashion information on model dolls reached a peak during the reigns of Louis XIV (1643–1715), Louis XV (1715–1774), and Louis XVI (1774–1792) when Versailles was the criterion of royal courts. The other courts of Europe were so hungry for this information that the dolls were rushed in fast coaches as far as the Russian city of St. Petersburg. Even war did not stop these inanimate fashion emissaries. In an article titled "Fashion Dolls and Their History" in *The Antiquarian* (December 1929), Elizabeth B. Hurlock says: "When England and France were at war, the English ports were closed to all outsiders, but were open to the Grand Courier de la Mode, a huge alabaster fashion doll from Paris."

The first French dressmaker to achieve fame and "name" status was Rose Bertin (1747-1813) during the reign of Louis XVI and Marie Antoinette. Good business woman that she was, Mademoiselle Bertin sent her own dolls to the capitals of Europe to solicit orders for her shop in the Rue St. Honoré. As the dolls traveled all over Europe, so did Rose's fame until she was nicknamed "Minister of Fashion."

It is easy to see how the French model dolls established France's fashion leadership, beginning with Queen Isabella's unique idea at the end of the fourteenth century. The doll custom flourished during Rose Bertin's time.

Life-sized dolls from France and England provided Colonial America with its major means of keeping up to date on fashion trends. When the "fashion babies" (as they were called here) arrived after a long ocean voyage, the local dressmakers hastened to copy them for their well-to-do customers.

Vogue's Doll Fashion Show

Vogue, which bowed on December 17, 1892 as a weekly "journal of society, fashion, and the ceremonial side of life," sponsored the first doll fashion show in America in 1896, featuring fashions by New York dressmakers. (The first show of this kind had just taken place with "extraordinary success" in London.) *Vogue's* "Model Doll Show," given as a benefit in Sherry's large ballroom on March 20-23, opened with a fashionable private preview attended by more than 1000 persons. Among the 63 socially prominent patronesses were such society leaders as Mrs. John Jacob Astor, Mrs. August Belmont, and Mrs. William Rhinelander Stewart. With tickets at 50 cents, $500 was raised at the opening. (Compare this modest sum with current benefit fashion shows that raise from $50,000 to $100,000 at one performance.)

The March 26, 1896 issue of *Vogue,* in reporting the success of the event, gave a hint of the status of American fashion:

"In this setting more than one hundred and fifty dolls, as miniature fashion figures were shown in wonderful variety of color and costume, and carried out much more effectively than the most sanguine wishes had pictured the original idea, as conceived by *Vogue,* of a worthy expression of dress by leading American dressmakers.

"The Model Doll Show, under the management of *Vogue,* gives New York dressmakers the first recognition that their merits deserve, and accords to them a position from which they have long been excluded by the indiscriminating laudation for so many years bestowed on London and Paris.

Model Doll Show

UNDER THE MANAGEMENT OF VOGUE

IN AID OF

THE SCARLET FEVER AND DIPHTHERIA HOSPITAL

SHERRY'S, MARCH 20TH, 21ST AND 23D

THE Show will be opened with a Private View, Friday, 20 March, at 3 o'clock, and continue on Saturday, 21 March, and Monday 23 March. The extraordinary feature will be dolls dressed as models of special costumes and of prevailing fashions. These dolls will be dressed by the leading designers of New York, and present a great variety of subject and treatment.

TICKETS   -   -   -   FIFTY CENTS

PATRONESSES:

Mrs. Charles B. Alexander	Mrs. Richard H. Derby	Mrs. Eugene Kelly	Mrs. C. Albert Stevens
Miss Malvina Appleton	Mrs. Arthur M. Dodge	Mrs. Edward King	Mrs. William Rhinelander Stewart
Mrs. John Jacob Astor	Mrs. Cleveland H. Dodge	Mrs. Gustav Kissel	Mrs. Joseph Stickney
Mrs. Charles T. Barney	Mrs. John R. Drexel	Mrs. Luther Kountze	Mrs. T. Suffern Tailer
Miss de Barril	Mrs. Nicholas Fish	Mrs. Charles Lanier	Mrs. Henry A. C. Taylor
Mrs. Edmund L. Baylies	Miss de Forest	Mrs. J. Lawrence Lee	Mrs. Jonathan Thorne
Mrs. August Belmont	Mrs. George B. de Forest	Mrs. Edward A. Le Roy, Jr.	Mrs. Henry Graff Trevor
Mrs. David Wolfe Bishop	Miss Furniss	Mrs. Charles H. Marshall	Mrs. John B. Trevor
Mrs. Heber R. Bishop	Mrs. John Lyon Gardiner	Mrs. Ogden Mills	Mrs. Paul Tuckerman
Mrs. William T. Blodgett	Mrs. Elbridge T. Gerry	Mrs. John W. Minturn	Mrs. Arthur Turnure
Mrs. James A. Burden	Mrs. G. G. Haven	Mrs. Trenor L. Park	Mrs. Cornelius Vanderbilt
Miss Callender	Mrs. Peter Cooper Hewitt	Mrs. James W. Pinchot	Mrs. F. W. Vanderbilt
Mrs. A. Cass Canfield	Mrs. Thomas Hitchcock	Mrs. George B. Post	Mrs. William Seward Webb
Mrs. Henry E. Coe	Mrs. G. G. Howland	Mrs. M. Taylor Pyne	Mrs. Geo. Peabody Wetmore
Mrs. Joseph H. Choate	Mrs. Edward W. Humphreys	Mrs. Jules Reynal	Mrs. John C. Wilmerding
Mrs. H. H. Curtis	Mrs. Morris K. Jesup	Mrs. T. J. Oakley Rhinelander	Mrs. Orme Wilson
Mrs. Brockholst Cutting	Mrs. William Jay	Mrs. Sidney Dillon Ripley	Mrs. Buchanan Winthrop
Miss Cuyler	Mrs. Walter Jennings	Mrs. Henry Sloane	Mrs. Frank Spencer Witherbee
Mrs. Francis Delafield	Mrs. Frederic R. Jones	Mrs. William Douglas Sloane	

Further particulars, if desired, will be supplied by the management,

VOGUE, 154 FIFTH AVENUE, NEW YORK.

Full-page announcement of "Model Doll Show" from *Vogue* Magazine, March 12, 1896. Courtesy of The Condé Nast Publications.

"The Model Doll Show is a step in the direction of destroying the false idea that Paris leads New York in fashions for Americans."

THE FIRST LIVE FASHION SHOWING

The story of the beginning of the French couture by Charles Frederick Worth, an Englishman born at Bourne in 1826, is not only fascinating but also includes the next step in the development of showing fashions. After working during his teens with fabrics and clothes in several London shops, Worth embarked for Paris around 1845. Here his second job was with Gagelin & Opigez who sold cashmere shawls and ready-made coats, as well as fabrics and trimmings. Working as a *demoiselle de magazin* (shopgirl) in the same shop was an attractive young woman named Marie Vernet. Young Worth soon drafted her to put on the shawls to show customers how they looked when worn. Marie thus became the first live model.

In the course of time, Mademoiselle Vernet became Madame Worth and the young husband began to design dresses and hats for her and have them made at the shop. Customers admired the designs so much that Worth was permitted to open a made-to-order department where they could select designs in muslin to be translated in their personal selections of fabric and trimmings.

About 1858 Worth left Gagelin and opened the first real couture house, together with a Swede named Bobergh as partner. The shop was located at 7 Rue de la Paix and launched this area as the center of the early couture houses.

The First Mannequins are Born

In his new house, Worth made a practice of showing his clothes on live mannequins, who were usually English. When not modeling the collection, these attractive young women wore high-necked, long-sleeved black dresses cut in the latest fashion. (This is probably how the black dress as a uniform for saleswomen originated.)

The word "mannequin," meaning someone who wears a garment to show how it looks, was first used at the House of Worth. A reporter for *La Vie Parisienne* visited Worth one day with a companion who asked to have someone put on a dress so she could see the effect. A *vendeuse* obliged. The reporter later wrote an article about the visit, titling it, "Entrée de Mlle. Mannequin." Until that time, the word "mannequin" referred only to a dummy or dress stand.

Worth also used the dispatching of dressed dolls, now in smaller sizes, to obtain orders from other countries.

THE FRENCH COUTURE ADOPTS THE MANNEQUIN

Before the end of the nineteenth century, a number of other couture houses opened in Paris and the showing of clothes on mannequins became the usual thing. The couturiers frequently dressed their mannequins in the fashions of the house and sent them out to spots where fashionable and wealthy people gathered in order to foster the wearing of new fashions and to promote the name of the house. One favorite place for parading clothes was the racetrack at Longchamps.

The colorful and inventive Paul Poiret, who opened his own couture house in 1904, made history when he took live mannequins to foreign countries to show his clothes instead of sending fashion dolls. It was reported that his arrival in Russia with nine mannequins caused such a furore that he had to lock them in their hotel rooms every night for safety.

The Contributions of Patou

Two innovations in showing clothes are attributed to Jean Patou. Although the press had been coming to Paris since 1910, and *Vogue* had even reported on Paris fashions several years before that, Patou staged the first special preview showing for the press on the evening before one of his regular openings in 1921.

Three years later, Patou caused a stir in Paris by bringing over six American girls to model his collection. Inspired by an American customer who complained that she couldn't visualize how the clothes modeled by French mannequins would look on an American figure, he came to *Vogue* in New York for help in selecting American models to show his clothes in Paris. Edna Woolman Chase, *Vogue*'s editor at the time, describes in her autobiography "Always in *Vogue*" how 500 assorted females rushed to answer the advertisement they read in the newspapers in November 1924:

"A Paris couturier desires to secure three ideal types of beautiful young American women who seriously desire careers as mannequins in our Paris atelier. Must be smart, slender, with well shaped feet and ankles and refined of manner. Sail within three weeks. Attractive salary proposition, one year's contract and traveling expenses paid both ways. Selection to be made by a jury at the offices of *Vogue*, 14th floor, 19 West 44th Street. Apply Friday morning ten to ten-thirty." [Reprinted by permission of Doubleday & Company.]

One of the most distinguished juries ever to select a group of models met at the Ritz-Carlton Hotel in New York to view the semifinalists.

Mrs. Chase, Elsie de Wolfe, Edward Steichen, Condé Nast, and Patou narrowed the group to six girls as the lucky winners of this unique assignment instead of the three girls originally called for. The six American beauties who set out for Paris were Lillian Farley (who used the name Dinarzade when modeling), Josephine Armstrong, Dorothy Raynor, Carolyn Putnam, Edwina Prue, and Rosalind Stair.

It took a lot of diplomacy to make this glamorous group acceptable in Paris where news of Patou's importation was received as an insult to the French mannequins. To ward off a war of mannequins, he sent an emissary to meet the boat on which the girls arrived in order to teach them how to meet the press.

The Americans came through like experienced diplomats and charmed the full-dress audience on the opening night of the next collection. Patou used showmanship and humor to break the ice by beginning the showing with a parade of all his mannequins—French and American—wearing the simple little wrappers or smocks that were their uniforms in the *cabines* (dressing rooms) between fittings and showings. This clever trick homogenized the group.

It was these young women "refined of manner" who gave the cachet of acceptability to modeling as a profession or career. Until this time, the mannequins had been selected entirely from the working classes who had little rapport with the elegant couture customers.

AMERICA INVENTS THE LIVE FASHION SHOW

Although Edna Woolman Chase, editor of *Vogue* from 1914 to 1954, claims to have originated the live fashion show in 1914, trade fashion shows took place before this time in the several midwestern fashion manufacturing centers of the United States. These trade shows began around 1910. They were given to promote the merchandise of the individual manufacturers and to publicize the cities as fashion markets.

"The Greatest Style Show in the World"

Perhaps the first big spectacular show was "The Greatest Style Show in the World" given by the Chicago Garment Manufacturers' Association on August 18, 1914 in the new Medinah Temple in Chicago before almost 5000 persons who were attending the semiannual market. Besides the elaborate fashion presentation in 9 scenes of 250 garments modeled by "100 shapely women," news was made by the filming of the show. At a dress rehearsal the day before, the production was recorded on 7000 feet of film so that merchants throughout the United States could have the film shown in local theaters.

According to the August 18th edition of *Women's Wear Daily*, this was the "largest interior picture ever attempted. Forty lights of 5000 candle power each, besides the house lights, were used to produce the pictures, which will give the retailers and others throughout the country an opportunity to see the $32,500 scenic and fashion production." [Reprinted by permission of *Women's Wear Daily*.]

The Chicago show is of special interest for two other reasons. The presentation took place on the huge 70 by 100 foot stage and also employed a large platform that extended out into the audience. It is possible that this was the first use of a "runway" to bring clothes closer to the viewers at a fashion show.

The other item of special interest is the very slow tempo of the modeling. While the show was presented in situation scenes, each model had one minute and twenty seconds to walk to the front of the stage and show her outfit. The audience probably didn't get home until morning after that show!

The Chicago Show of 1917

Another history-making trade fashion show took place in Chicago in 1917. This was "The Land of Vogue" staged by the Chicago Garment Manufacturers' Association from February 5 to 10 at the Strand Theatre. The presentation featured a new technique that was later used extensively in the 1960s—that of showing movie footage to set a background scene for live models. For example, the first scene, "The Dawn of 1917," opened with a view of snow on the screen, quickly dissolving into a "picture of daisies with a vision of the Orient in the background." The movie screen then lifted to reveal an Oriental setting.

THE FIRST FASHION SHOW FOR THE PUBLIC

When Paris fashion was suddenly cut off from the United States in August 1914 with France's involvement in World War I, Edna Woolman Chase faced her first big challenge as the new editor of *Vogue*. Riding along atop a Fifth Avenue bus in New York, she was wondering how to fill the fashion gap when the idea of sponsorship of American fashions struck her. Remembering the doll shows of *Vogue*, she visualized a fashion exhibition sponsored by society leaders for the benefit of some worthy wartime cause.

With the support of Henri Bendel, who owned the smartest shop in the city and included the top socialites among his customers, and of Mrs. Stuyvesant Fish, a social leader, she was able to put over the idea. Mrs. Fish became the magnet for attracting a formidable list of patronesses that included such names as Mrs. Vincent Astor and Mrs. August Belmont.

Together with Mrs. Chase and Helen Koues of *Vogue*, seven fashionable society leaders composed the committee to select the clothes. The event was christened the "Fashion Fête" and opened with a big gala on the evening of November 4, 1914 in the ballroom of the chic Ritz-Carlton Hotel. Additional performances were given in the afternoon and evening of the next two days.

The opening performance began with a dinner, after which the guests filed into the ballroom that had been set up as a theater. During the evening, debutantes sold programs and chances on outfits exhibited on live models. Dancing followed the show. The proceeds went to the Committee of Mercy to benefit widows and orphans of the Allies.

Vogue's Reportage of the Fête

A feeling of the time and the occasion comes through in *Vogue's* stories about the show. An article in the November 1st issue was headlined:

THE STORY OF THE FASHION FÊTE
With Paris Sorely Stricken, and All Possible European Successors in Like Plight, New York Has Thrust upon It the Honor of Designing Fashions, and so, in the Manner of Paris, Will Hold Its First Great Fashion Opening

Emily Post covered the Fashion Fête in the December 1st issue in a feature with an equally long headline:

WHERE FASHIONABLES AND FASHION MET
When the Footlights Flared up upon the Fashion Fête, They Illuminated not only the Fashions New York Had Created for that Gala Night, but also an Audience that Attested how Important to Society Are These Fashions

This story included a description of the show itself. The curtain opened on two well-known singers of the day—Mrs. Ray Dennis, playing the role of "Miss Vogue," and Andres de Segurola of the Metropolitan Opera as an artist. This was the opening dialogue:

"Ah, Miss Vogue, what a surprise. I called on the chance of finding you, but thought you would be in Europe with your sisters of the Red Cross.

"Oh, you see, my friend, I found I was much more needed here.

"Here? And what for?

"To look after the fashions, of course."

Photograph copyrighted by Baumann

Four young socialites, who ushered at an afternoon performance of the *Vogue* Fashion
Fête, hold little silk and lace muffs into which they tucked the proceeds from selling pro-
grams. Reprinted from *Vogue* Magazine, December 1, 1914, by permission from The
Condé Nast Publications.

The artist then ridiculed the New York fashions, saying, "There is not a decent frock in the whole town." Miss Vogue made a bet that he was mistaken and the showing of fashions opened, divided into groups. Miss Vogue announced the maker of each garment as the model entered. The mannequins pivoted on the stage and then descended steps to the ballroom floor to walk through the audience. By the time the show ended, American fashion had proved itself.

This Fashion Fête marked the beginning of a new form of entertainment for the public — the fashion show — and gave it a social cachet.

OTHER FASHION SHOW MILESTONES

There have been so many and such varied fashion shows in the more than half century since the Fashion Fête of 1914 that all of them could never be documented. However, there are several shows that were significant for one reason or another and deserve mention.

The Fashion Battle of Zurich

In 1918, with Europe still in turmoil after World War I, fashion waged its own little war. The dressmakers or couturiers of Vienna toured a showing of their work to Zurich, Switzerland. Redfern of the Paris couture was so incensed by this affront to the international one-upmanship of French fashion that he organized a show with other members of the French couture and personally took it to Zurich on November 9th, two days before the Armistice on November 11th. It is reported that the fighting Frenchmen easily won the fashion victory.

An American in Paris

Not often has American fashion dared to invade Paris. It took plucky Elizabeth Hawes to try it at a Fourth of July showing in 1931. She booked Les Ambassadeurs, a night club, for a tea-time and an evening performance to show French dressmakers "what American women want in the way of clothes."

Although Miss Hawes produced the show with her typical verve and enthusiasm, the show simply didn't come off well. In the first place, she found that her American fashions were not dramatic enough to stand up in a night club atmosphere. Second, the French press snubbed the show, in spite of its novelty, for fear of antagonizing the French designers.

The Men Model Clothes

Six years after her foray into French territory, in February 1937, Elizabeth Hawes scored another first by showing men's clothes along with women's. She persuaded a New York tailor, Tony Williams, to join her in an evening party at which they would both exhibit their clothes, plus some special ones for men that she would do and he would make.

Miss Hawes chose six prominent New York men and designed suits that each agreed to model. Her celebrated group consisted of a young man-about-town, a lawyer, a drama critic, a stage designer, a dancer, and an advertising executive. To assure complete cooperation, she assigned a pretty female model to be responsible for escorting each man through his modeling assignment. Each model was cautioned not to let her man escape, except over her dead body. To put the male models in the proper mood, Miss Hawes sent each one a bottle of champagne several hours before the party. Only one man got cold feet and literally had to be dragged to the platform by his guardian model.

The Fashion Group Shows

One of the most distinguished women's organizations in the world is The Fashion Group, which was founded in New York in February 1931 by 75 women fashion executives. It is now an international organization with almost 5000 members in 31 Regional Groups throughout the world. One of the objectives is to provide a central source of information on fashion trends. To accomplish this, The Fashion Group undertook fashion-trend shows for its members and guests almost from the beginning.

The first big Fashion Group spectacular was "Fashion Futures" on the evening of September 11, 1935 in the Hotel Astor in New York. Over 1200 members of the press and fashion industry viewed the show. A Fashion Group Bulletin reported: "Fashion Futures, the first un-propaganda, un-commercial and un-subsidized fashion show ever presented, sets a new standard for the entire fashion world, as well as providing a colorful new chapter in the success story of The Fashion Group."

The fashions shown were selected from "creators, importers, and retailers from 57th Street to 34th Street." Accessories were provided by the foremost manufacturers. All were shown anonymously, with no names given in the program or by the commentator.

An amusing incident, reported in The Fashion Group Bulletin, reveals that producing a fashion show was as hectic then as it is today: "When the melee was at its height in The Fashion Group office — models dressing, imports being unpacked, committee making decisions, people waiting to get tickets, Mrs. Kremer (the executive director) answered a phone, writing a ticket reservation and eating a sandwich all at once — when a bespectacled gentleman calmly approached Mrs. Kremer and said he wished to talk to her about the necessity of business women carrying adequate accident and health insurance!"

"Fashion Futures" was enlarged in September 1936 with clothes from New York, Paris, London, and Hollywood. About 1500 tickets were sold for the fashion parade and late supper. The Fashion Group called itself "the only organization to attempt this unique unsponsored fashion presentation, completely free from propaganda for any cause or organization."

Ruth Carson, in a *Collier's* article of October 17, 1936 titled "Your First Look," described the excitement of this glamour-packed evening:

"Out front the lights grow dim in the silver-and-gold ballroom of the Waldorf. From around the tables of ten that pack the floor and balconies, the white-tied and jeweled audience turns toward the stage. The orchestra strikes up, the curtains part, and the greatest fashion show in the world is on. The greatest and the best. Because it is put on by fashion experts whose year-round job it is to design, select, edit, purchase and sell clothes. They know their stuff.

". . . The best clothes in the world are here, on the best fashion models in the world, girls whose faces you have seen on magazine covers and in the ads, girls with an eye on Hollywood and Hollywood's eye on them." [Reprinted by permission of Crowell Collier Publishing Company.]

The Board of Governors of the fashion history-making organization voted in 1937 "to hold the most important fashion show America has ever seen, the Fashion Futures — American Edition. It will dramatize the great part that the American producer plays in the adaptation of fashion to the American scene." Staged on November 22, 1937, this mammoth effort included 700 dresses, hats, furs, suits, and other fashions worn by 106 models on 2 stages in 22 scenes.

Quoting again from a Fashion Group Bulletin describing this show: "Full of promotional material and ideas and setting a new tempo for fashion shows in America. . . . Action and dialogue were used throughout the entire production, which approached the dimensions of a musical show. The 'Big Apple,' called America's first folk dance was the climax of the scene, in which 48 mannequins in four different shades of blue illustrated America's prime talent, 'America Dresses the Millions.'"

It is interesting to note that it required 168 members working on 13 committees to bring off the event, illustrating that a fashion show is a production. These were the committees:

Directing   Promotion
Planning   Arrangement

Selection   Hostesses
Fashion Jury   Patrons
Production   Tickets
Printed Program   Photography Selection
                                   Press

In 1941 Fashion Futures took place in both New York and Los Angeles. The New York version played on two nights, January 8 and 9, to 3500 persons, with Mayor Fiorello LaGuardia as honorary chairman. An innovation was a competition among beauties from four cities for the title "Miss Fashion Futures." The Fashion Group Bulletin reported: "We rivaled the town's best musicals in stage sets, lighting, drama, gorgeous girls, and in cost of production too. We spent $47,000 on that show — $13,000 for mannequins alone. . . ."

On the West Coast, the Los Angeles and San Francisco groups joined forces in Los Angeles on February 13, 1941 for their version of "Fashion Futures" at a dinner in the Ambassador Hotel attended by 1000 persons. Film star Reginald Gardiner was master of ceremonies, assisted by a different commentator for each of the five scenes depicting American life. Movie columnist Hedda Hopper commentated one scene, while a racetrack announcer commentated the Santa Anita scene. It was a star-studded night: $250,000 worth of clothes by West Coast film and other designers were adorned with $2 million worth of diamonds, and modeled by 75 professionals, socialites, and movie starlets.

The Fashion Group has produced many other successful fashion shows — some large, some small. On September 11, 1935 they held their first fashion meeting in New York to analyze and show fashions from the Paris couture. A candid-camera film of current events was a backup for this program. These Paris couture shows have grown to such importance that they are now presented twice in one day at a breakfast and lunch showing viewed by about 3500 persons. They are held in March, to cover the spring showings, and in September for fall.

Today The Fashion Group of New York has a major schedule of fashion showings open to members and their guests. In addition to Paris couture meetings, there are spring and fall American fashion shows, seasonal fabric and color shows, children's shows, sportswear shows, home furnishings programs, and special shows such as a California presentation, a Scandinavian show, and a Mexican meeting to show fashions originating in these areas.

Each of the Regional Groups plans its own appropriate meetings and shows, many of which are major undertakings.

To accent the season's important color, burgundy, The Fashion Group uses a background of wine glasses, bottles, and carafes on shelves stretching the breadth of the stage, 1964. Courtesy of The Fashion Group.

As a foil for Saint Laurent fashions inspired by the painter Mondrian, an abstract background in white fronted by a bank of steps makes the stark setting for The Fashion Group's fall import show, 1965. Courtesy of The Fashion Group.

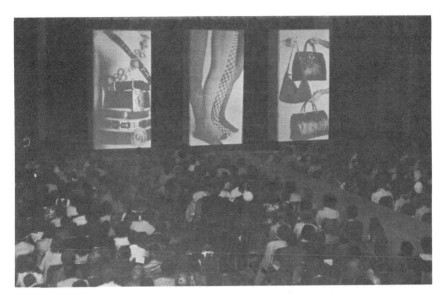

To dramatize American fall fashions, The Fashion Group, in 1969, fills the stage with three huge white slabs onto which details and accessories are projected between sequences. Courtesy of The Fashion Group.

Models pose against the abstract stage setting at The Fashion Group's American showing. Courtesy of The Fashion Group.

As a kicky young setting for its show, "What Is Young," in 1969, The Fashion Group asked a group of artists to design sliding screens which opened for the models' entry. A different screen slid onstage to introduce each scene. Courtesy of the Fashion Group.

The Fashion Show Flourishes

From the 1920s on, everyone was getting into the fashion act.

There were radio fashion shows like the benefit that fashion authority Tobé hostessed. Her first was "A Spring Cocktail" on March 7, 1934 in the Grand Ballroom of the Ritz-Carlton Hotel in New York. As she broadcast the live show over the Columbia network, the same show was being enacted simultaneously in twelve cities across the country. This was so successful that a follow-up "Diary of a Deb" was given on October 10th of the same year.

The Century of Progress Exhibition in Chicago, a kind of world's fair, spawned a whole school of fashion shows during the summers of 1933 and 1934 when it ran. Mrs. Ford Carter conducted the shows for thousands of spectators. *Good Housekeeping* staged fashion shows in the garden of the pavilion of its exhibit Garden House.

Shows were given for entertainment on ships at sea. Hollywood movie studios publicized films by sponsoring showings of costumes. Popular books provided themes, such as the society dinner dance and fashion show in 1936 in Washington, D.C., featuring "Van Gogh" prints by Celanese and inspired by the publication of Irving Stone's biography of Vincent Van Gogh, *Lust for Life.*

Great Spectaculars of the 1940s

For a number of years, beginning in 1942, *The New York Times* produced a spectacular fashion show appropriately named "Fashions of the Times." Originated by Virginia Pope, then fashion editor of the newspaper, it was professionally staged in Times Hall, a 500-seat theater, and ran for several performances each year in October or November. The show never failed to set important new fashion trends. The goal was to establish the *Times* as a fashion authority, and thus to attract fashion advertising. A special fashion supplement in the Sunday edition of the *Times* was introduced in 1946 at the time of the show and continued in succeeding years. In magazine format, it reported the show and carried fashion advertising. "Fashions of the Times" was last produced in 1950, but the supplement continued as a special fashion magazine twice a year in the spring and fall.

Eleanor Lambert, a well-known New York public relations and publicity consultant, came on the scene in the early 1940s as a talented fashion-show producer. Her innovation was the use of celebrities worked into a show by an especially written script. She initiated the annual Coty American Fashion Critics' Awards shows in 1943. The next year, in 1944, she staged a milestone show in the Astor Hotel as the opener for the first semiannual Press Week sponsored by New York Dress Institute for fashion and women's-page editors from newspapers across the country. In a presidential election year, it was called the "CHIC Show" (Convention Honoring Inexpensive Clothes) and featured fashions not over $50 retail to publicize the great New York market. Lester Gaba, probably the greatest fashion-show director of all time, staged this show, which began his long association with Miss Lambert. Together they produced some of the most celebrated fashion shows during the next twenty-five years.

A famous series of shows produced by the Lambert and Gaba team was the annual benefit luncheons for The National Foundation's "March of Dimes" from 1945 through 1960. Set in the Grand Ballroom of the Waldorf-Astoria Hotel, fashion themes were presented in glamorous scenes with top celebrities modeling, performing, or commentating. Helen Hayes, Ethel Merman, Jose Ferrer, and Carol Burnett are but a few of the big names who contributed their time and talent for this cause. Every show was a feast for celebrity-watchers, and every show crystallized certain fashion trends.

The first "March of Dimes" show set the standard for those to come. Columnist Inez Robb wrote the script. Noted commentators were from the movies and theater: Leonora Corbett, Mary Astor, and Louis Calhern. Alicia Markova danced, and Mary Martin was one of the cele-

An Adele Simpson design for the "business glamour girl," being modeled at the sixth annual Coty American Fashion Critics' Awards fashion show, 1948. Courtesy of Coty.

brated models. The following year, Arlene Francis, Gertrude Lawrence, and Brian Aherne commentated. George Balanchine created and directed a special ballet for the show titled "Resurgence," and also starred in the number. Among other big names that made appearances that year were Danny Kaye, Gypsy Rose Lee, and Bess Myerson. It would be hard, ever again, to recapture the glamour of those shows.

New York City's Big Show

What could have been more appropriate to celebrate New York's Golden Anniversary of the consolidation of 5 boroughs and 27 cities into Greater New York than a fashion show at the Golden Anniversary Exposition in Grand Central Palace that ran from August 23 to September 19, 1948. The theme of the Exposition interpreted New York as the capital of the world, including the fashion world.

At 8:30 each evening, a parade of 100 models dressed in fashions representing the whole New York apparel market descended a spiraling golden ramp. A special feature was 20 ballet dancers wearing the Jubilee Dress — a black taffeta shirtwaist dress with gold Lurex stripes, priced at under $20 and made by Henry Rosenfeld, one of the big volume dress manufacturers of the time. One entire scene was in gold. Cosmetics and accessories were highlighted in separate sequences.

The show was climaxed by a bridal scene of five brides representing the five boroughs and a Golden Jubilee bride — all descending the golden ramp on the arms of six handsome fathers-of-the-bride.

MARY QUANT UPDATES THE FASHION SHOW

The 1960s saw a complete revolution in the fashion show — actually the first big change since the early shows at the beginning of the cen-

Ballet number during the "March of Dimes" fashion show, 1946. The simple stage setting in the Grand Ballroom of the Waldorf-Astoria features an oversized fashion figure. Courtesy of The National Foundation — March of Dimes.

Noted actress Gertrude Lawrence is one of the celebrity models in the second "March of Dimes" fashion show, 1946. Courtesy of The National Foundation — March of Dimes.

tury. Credit is given to young London designer Mary Quant for starting the new trend. The occasion was the press opening in 1958 of her second boutique in London: Knightsbridge Bazaar. Although Mary Quant was already a pacesetter and the originator of Mod fashions for London's young "birds," she had never had a press showing and hardly knew what one was. An editor of English *Vogue* convinced her that she should have one to let the world know about her fashion pioneering.

Mary Quant persuaded nine top photographic models to appear in the show because she believed they had an ability to move about in clothes, while the usual fashion show model simply paraded. She wanted to show her designs in action, worn by living, breathing people.

Taped music opened the show and blasted forth to the end. From a little balcony above the shop's first floor, the models danced down the stairs to where the press audience was standing. Concealed wind machines kept the clothes in motion. Everything was totally accessorized for the occasion for which it was intended. With a Norfolk jacket and knickers, appropriate for shooting, the model carried a shotgun and swung a dead pheasant purchased from nearby Harrods. Believability was carried a bit too far when blood from the thawing bird splattered the walls.

With party dresses the girls whirled (and perhaps wove a bit) with an oversized glass of champagne in hand. (Mary believes a glass of champagne for every model before the show makes them sparkle.) And not a single word of commentary was spoken.

In her book *Quant by Quant*, the young designer describes the show's impact: "No one had seen anything like this before. No one had ever before used this style of showing in London or anywhere else. People

Ballerina Vera Zorina whirls onto the runway in the "March of Dimes" fashion show, 1946. Courtesy of The National Foundation—March of Dimes.

Bess Myerson, former Miss America, wears an evening ensemble in the "March of Dimes" show, 1946. Courtesy of The National Foundation — March of Dimes.

were heard to say, 'The Method School of Modelling has arrived' and things like, 'This is the wackiest show ever . . . and the funniest!'" [Reprinted by permission of Cassell & Co. Limited and G. P. Putnam's Sons. Copyright © by Mary Quant.]

This show brought in a new era in fashion shows that developed during the 1960s and became the new way: dancing and movement instead of the mannequin's traditional walk, sound throughout, and no commentary. In the mid-1960s slides and movie projection were added as an integral part of the fashion show or as background.

THE PROJECTED FASHION SHOW ON FILM

Since the film or movie made a big comeback in the 1960s as popular entertainment, especially for teens and college students, it follows that the fashion show on film was a natural step in the development of fash-

Danny Kaye provides star quality for the "March of Dimes" fashion show, 1946. Courtesy of The National Foundation — March of Dimes.

Mary Quant, young London designer and boutique owner, who created a new approach to the fashion show. Courtesy of Mary Quant.

ion shows. Although this is not the first time film has been used to record a show, it represents the greatest development to date of this means of presenting fashion.

Paris couturier Paul Poiret recorded in his autobiography, *King of Fashion*, that he brought a fashion film of his own making to the United States on his first visit. He was shocked when censors prohibited the showing of the film as obscene because of the short skirts worn—just above the ankle. There was also the Chicago fashion film of 1914, already described.

Norma Geer, fashion director of Celanese Fibers Company until her death in the mid-1960s, saw in the year 1960 the excitement that film could lend to fashion. To promote the use of crepe fabrics in fashion (Celanese makes acetate, one of the fibers in rayon and acetate crepe), she conceived "Star in Crepe," a dramatic high-fashion film. This was produced by Columbia Pictures with all the drama that Hollywood techniques could give. Edith Head designed special fashions, Nelson Riddle provided the music score, and John Engstead was the photographer. Released in 1961, it ran for three years in stores, at press shows, and on television across the country.

Seeing the interest of young people in films, Norma Geer then supervised the making of a charming half-hour film, "Fantasy in Fortrel," in cooperation with *Seventeen* Magazine whose fashion editors served as consultants. This also was shot on the Columbia lot in Hollywood by John Engstead. The movie followed a story in which the star, model Terry Reno, traveled from scene to scene by balloon, helicopter, or other means, as a device for moving from one fashion sequence to the next. Fashions were especially designed in Celanese fabrics by junior manufacturers in the New York market.

A gala premiere for the press and store buyers was given in the Grand Ballroom of the Plaza Hotel in New York. After the film was screened, star Terry Reno led live models down the runway in the fashions featured in the film. This movie was successfully shown in 1962 in stores where the fashions were available and on television.

The first young fashion movie with a rock beat was the color film "Youthquake" that Paul Young—then head of Youthquake (junior fashions)—had made in London in 1963. The camera followed a group of young English "swingers" about town. Action was fast, with the young models (male and female) racing from one contemporary scene and activity to another. A rock sound track took the place of commentary. Not one word was spoken.

Following this, a number of other fashion movies were made, usually commissioned by a large fiber company or manufacturer that could afford to pay the extremely high costs involved.

An exotic scene from the filmed fashion show "Basic Black" being coached by director William Claxton. Courtesy of Claxton Productions.

Slide shows incorporating new projection techniques and using multiple projectors and screens were created as a slightly less expensive, but effective, means of showing fashion. From this, slides and film footage combined with sound evolved into exciting staging backgrounds for live shows.

William Claxton and his wife, model Peggy Moffitt, have been responsible for several of the most contemporary and original fashion-

The same scene during the filming, with William Claxton directing from the camera area. Peggy Moffitt, center, performed in the film. Courtesy of Claxton Productions.

show movies. Their first was an experimental film "Basic Black," a sophisticated high fashion effort, made in 1966 with the cooperation of Rudi Gernreich who provided the clothes. Their purpose was to prove that fashion is an exciting subject for entertainment on film.

The Claxtons contributed toward the creative side of a shoe film shown at the Metropolitan Museum when Herbert and Beth Levine were given a Fashion Critics' Award. Extremely successful was their male fashion movie made in 1968 for Trevira, titled "Man in the Trevira Era."

The film may become the favorite fashion medium of the future. It combines sight and sound, offers tremendous scope, permits exciting camera "tricks," and is the favorite subject of identity for the young. The only deterrent may be the exceptionally high price of making a fashion show on film.

3

The Types of Fashion Shows and What They Accomplish

Every fashion show is staged by some individual, business, or organization to accomplish a specific goal. The types of shows that may be staged are categorized here by these goals of accomplishment.

THE SHOW TO SELL MERCHANDISE TO CONSUMERS

1. Retail Department and Specialty Store Shows

The fashion show has become such an effective selling tool for retail stores that it is an everyday occurrence. In fact, there are so many retail-store shows that they probably add up to more than the total of all other fashion shows. During a peak selling period, a store may give as many as six or seven shows within one day, spanning all size ranges and ages. During an entire year, the number of shows produced may reach 500. The fashion director of a store directs more shows in one year than a Broadway director does in a lifetime. In addition to direct selling, the store's aims may be:

- to introduce new fashions at the beginning of a season
- to introduce a new designer
- to show how to accessorize
- to demonstrate how to wear clothes and makeup
- to reach special groups of customers by showing merchandise they need, such as bridal, career, teen, college, children's, maternity, and men's and boys' clothes
- to maintain good public relations by staging pleasant, informative, and entertaining customer events
- to bring into the store potential customers for other merchandise

Shopping Center Shows. In the major shopping centers of the United States, the conglomerates of retail stores also produce fashion shows for customers. Most centers have a promotion director whose responsibility is to plan and stage events that will draw crowds to the center. The assumption is that the customers will then buy. The various stores in the center cooperate by providing clothes and accessories.

Joint Shows Downtown. Similarly a downtown association may spearhead a show in which all of the retailers participate, or may generate a promotion, leaving the fashion shows to the individual stores. This kind of excitement brings crowds of shoppers downtown and stimulates business for all stores in the area.

Oakland, California, used this means to attract young people downtown for their back-to-school shopping in August 1967. Merchants were faced with the problem of having their main shopping street torn up by the construction of a new subway. To motivate customers to withstand the unpleasantness of shopping in this situation, the merchants joined efforts in a major teen show.

The retailers of San Francisco, along with local designers, annually open the fall season with a gala outdoor fashion presentation in beautiful Union Square in the middle of the downtown shopping area. The giant show plays to thousands at noontime performances.

Showing on Television. Some successful television fashion shows have been produced by stores for special promotions. Macy's and Ohrbach's of New York were early users of the medium to introduce their collections of copies of couture imports. Both stores were striving to build a fashion image as well as to sell the clothes.

A few big department stores have successfully used local television shows for back-to-school and college promotions. The Boston Store of Milwaukee pioneered with a half-hour show in 1963 in order to expand their audience from the 1000 they could accommodate at a live show to an estimated 100,000 who could see it on television. Macy's of San Francisco began using television for their back-to-school fashions a year earlier, in 1962. Since teens are not big television viewers generally, Macy's announcement advertisements suggested soft drink parties to view the program. A coupon was provided so that teens could pick up a free four-pack of a soft drink and a big bag of potato chips at a grocery store as a starter for a party. Rich's of Atlanta adopted television for a very lively college show aired several times locally in August 1967.

The most ambitious back-to-school fashion show on television was produced by May-D & F of Denver in August 1969. A channel popular with young people was selected for a program that opened at 9:30 P.M. and continued until 4:00 A.M. Previously taped fashion sequences were interspersed with old movies, popular rock groups, and disc jockeys. Because of the night hours and the possibility of an audience of boys as well as girls (and also adults during the earlier hours), the show leaned heavily on entertainment.

During the period of the telecast, teen viewers were invited to call in and register for a prize drawing at the end of the show. Twenty young people answered the phones and handled over 11,000 calls. (It was reported that no one else in that telephone exchange was able to make or receive calls after 9:30!)

Because the show was designed to sell young fashions, the grand prize winner was announced in the store the following afternoon. Although the winner did not have to be present to receive the prize of a snow car, he or she could receive an additional prize of a trip to London if there. (She wasn't!)

More and more stores are learning to use mini-shows as television fashion commercials, but frequently these are institutional rather than of the fashion-merchandising nature because of the high costs involved. Fashion merchandise is difficult to exploit this way because it sells out relatively fast and thus makes an expensive commercial obsolescent. Another drawback to selling specific merchandise on television is the inability to see details and textures, the lack of color unless the commercial is broadcast and received in color, and the fleeting image that cannot be recalled by the viewer. A fashion-show technique may be used in an institutional commercial to publicize a store's wide selection of merchandise such as stockings or boots, where the merchandise shown is not easily identifiable.

2. Informal Modeling by Retail Stores

Another type of fashion-show appeal to consumers is the informal modeling of clothes. The majority of customers lack the imagination to visualize how clothes look on a body and how they should be worn and accessorized. Thus informal modeling is highly successful in selling merchandise.

Modeling in a tearoom or store restaurant is psychologically good. The customers are in a happy situation—sitting down, enjoying the company of a room full of other people, and eating. They are receptive to having a pretty model stop at the table and tell them about an outfit she is wearing. (The model must be provided with all pertinent information.) The audience is captive and cannot ignore the model or walk away.

Many stores and specialty shops employ models for a particular department or to walk through the store wearing new clothes from stock.

Although it is always worthwhile to get a customer to look at merchandise, this type of informal modeling is not as easy (and, possibly, not as successful) as tearoom modeling. In the first place, the model must wear clothing that is totally different from that worn by the customers so the the modeled clothes will stand out. For example, a model walking through a store in a fur coat might not be noticed at all if the customers are wearing coats and furs. On the other hand, a girl in an evening dress or a negligee would certainly stand out among winter-coated customers.

Second, customers shopping or rushing through a store are not inclined to stop and look at a model. Also most people are basically shy with strangers and won't ask questions.

Informal modeling within one department has an advantage over storewide modeling, since it reaches customers who are already interested in the particular classification of merchandise and are shopping for it. These customers will be inclined to stop and look at the model. There is a common interest between the two.

Occasionally a store ties in with a hotel dining room, a restaurant, or a club by providing informal modeling during lunch, tea, or cocktails. This gives the store additional exposure, publicity, and possible sales, while it provides entertainment for the guests. A number of restaurants in New York feature these shows at lunch on Wednesdays to attract women who want to meet before attending the mid-week theater matinees.

This kind of modeling has the same advantage that store, tearoom, or restaurant modeling has, but with the disadvantage that the audience is not in the store, and may never be. Thus potential resulting sales are questionable. Any store that provides clothes for this kind of modeling should be sure that the audience will be the type who would be likely to buy the clothes from both a taste and an economic standpoint.

3. Trunk Shows in Retail Stores

Still another type of consumer show is the trunk showing. Here a manufacturer or designer brings to the store most or all of his collection, theoretically in a trunk. He is usually stationed in or near the department where the merchandise is sold, with his fashions on hangers on a rack. At certain hours, his line is shown on models, or it may be informally modeled. The purpose is to give customers a chance to special-order clothes that are not stocked by the store.

A trunk showing may also take the form of a regular fashion show. It may be staged in the store's auditorium, tearoom, restaurant, or on the floor.

You are cordially
invited to our
Polly Flinders
Trunk Showing
of hand-smocked dresses.
Today, Tuesday, Wednesday

Meet the personal
representative from Polly Flinders,
who will be happy to help you
with your selection of transitional,
fall and early-holiday hand-smocked
dresses. And enter our drawing for a
free Polly Flinders dress wardrobe.
For infants through size 12. **7.00** to **16.00**

Liliputian Bazaar®, 5th Floor

Trunk Showing also at Garden City

Best & Co.

Fifth Avenue at Fifty First Street, New York

Advertisement by Best & Co. to publicize a trunk showing of little girls' dresses.

The trunk show has these distinct advantages for the store:

- It brings customers to the store and into the department involved.
- It gives customers a bigger selection and a feeling of receiving special treatment.

- The store enjoys extra sales without extra stock.
- When the trunk show is given by a top designer, there is prestige for the store in the personal appearance of a celebrity.

Several details are to be kept in mind when planning a trunk show in order to have it go smoothly. Time must be allocated for the clothes to be unpacked and ticketed with the store's retail price. Most important, the decision of who will fit models and line up the show has to be made in advance. This is ticklish because the designer may not arrive in time to do this preliminary work and may object to the way it was done when he does arrive.

An English designer arrived in one major store just as the first of three shows was going on (having stood up radio and television interviewers). At the end of the first show, she threw the staff and models into pandemonium by insisting that the models and lineup be changed before the next show an hour later. The store graciously complied, but not without tears. It is wise to be braced for this kind of emergency.

4. Couture and Made-to-Order Showings

The couturiers and made-to-order departments of stores have regular showings of their collections on models. This enables a customer to see all of the fashions offered, as they look when worn, and to make a choice of possible selections. After the showing, a customer may work with her *vendeuse* or saleslady and see again the numbers she has checked in order to make a final decision.

The couture, whether foreign or American, usually invites the press to a preview before opening a collection to customers.

Only a handful of made-to-order operations still exist in the United States because of the cost of doing this kind of business. The Paris couture represents the biggest concentration of made-to-order houses, but it, too, has had its difficulties because of costs and a change in the habits of the wealthy customers who support the couture. Younger women prefer to buy at least part of their wardrobes from ready-to wear stores or from interesting boutiques.

The majority of couturier and made-to-order showings have always been simple parades of models, usually one at a time. When Courrèges and Ungaro came on the scene in Paris in the mid-1960s as designers with contemporary young appeal, they enlivened their showings with rock music and dancing models, as well as appropriate staging.

THE SHOW TO SELL MERCHANDISE TO RETAILERS

1. Manufacturers' and Designers' Shows

Since a manufacturer is engaged in making merchandise to sell to a retail outlet, he is concerned with glamorizing his line or collection to make it as desirable to a buyer as possible and to top his competition. This calls for the showing of clothes on human bodies (good ones), properly accessorized, and presented with intelligence and flair. He, too, may want to show to the press.

The line is usually shown at specified times in his showroom, which has been built to accommodate these presentations. However, a manufacturer occasionally gives an opening show in a hotel, club, or other locale such as a theater. An example is the shows given by the big swimsuit makers of the West Coast. They introduce their new lines at their beautiful western showrooms or beside their pools, and then bring them to New York where they are shown to the press and New York buyers at parties in New York hotels.

As previously discussed, manufacturers produce trunk shows and, on occasion, provide their clothes for a civic, charitable, or other special event. The trunk shows are actually a means of selling to retailers without the stores' having to buy stock. The other shows are purely for public relations or publicity.

2. Trade Association Shows

The word "trade" as used in fashion refers to anything that occurs within the industry. It especially relates to the wholesale market or manufacturers. Thus there are "trade associations" made up of manufacturers of a certain classification of merchandise, such as the American Wood Council composed of wool growers, the Leather Industries of America made up of leather producers, or the Fur Information and Fashion Council whose members make fur coats and accessories. The primary purpose of these organizations is to promote the use of their particular products, to publicize their industry, and to disseminate information. A fashion presentation for retailers is a frequent medium for accomplishing these aims.

An example of this kind of effort is the spring and fall showings of hat fashions by the Millinery Institute at a gala dinner show for New York press and store buyers. The show is elaborately staged with the possible appearance of celebrities or entertainers. On the Sunday preceding this trade show, the Millinery Institute previews for the out-of-town and local press at a brunch. Excellent press kits of releases and pictures, plus a hatbox of favors for each editor, are provided.

Shows to Promote an Ingredient Product. Included in the trade-show category are the fashion shows given by companies that make ingredient products. An "ingredient product" is one that goes into a finished product, or into another ingredient that goes into a finished product. The fiber nylon is an example. This is made by a fiber producer, such as DuPont or Monsanto, who sells it to mills who weave it into fabrics. The fabric may be sold as a finished product for customers to buy by the yard, or it may be sold to a garment manufacturer as an ingredient for making a dress.

Major ingredient products in the fashion world are fibers and fabrics. Producers of these products give numerous fashion shows for retailers to promote their ingredients and to give publicity to their manufacturer-customers who have used the ingredients. When one has a fashion show, the thrust is threefold: promoting the fiber, the mill or converter (who finishes the fabric), and the garment manufacturer.

A trade fashion show for retail store buyers, using an astrology theme, is hosted by Du Pont at the Dallas Fashion Mart. Courtesy of Du Pont.

Retail store buyers are entertained by Du Pont at a Banlon nylon cruisewear show in the Du Pont Auditorium in New York. Courtesy of Du Pont.

The most famous of the ingredient shows are the Milliken Breakfast Shows given in the Grand Ballroom of the Waldorf-Astoria Hotel every morning for a period of about two weeks in May and June during the fall wholesale market period in New York. The show is an hour-long Broadway-type musical played by professional actors, singers, and dancers. Breakfast is served to a full house of 1800 store buyers and executives at 7 A.M. Split-second timing is maintained so that the curtain goes up at 8 o'clock and closes at 9 o'clock each morning, when a fleet of buses is waiting at the door to whisk the buyers off to their day's work in the market.

A breakfast-in-the-afternoon press preview precedes the opening of the breakfast shows, but the press is also welcome to attend any morning.

The Milliken Breakfast Show, in 1969, spoofs the son of the boss who tries to reorient the family store in the hippy image.

A production number featuring children's fashions, in the Milliken Breakfast Show, 1969.

Acapulco inspires a rousing musical finale to a Milliken Breakfast Show, 1969.

More than six months of preparation goes into the Milliken show. A complete book with lyrics is especially written. Fashion experts work with the entire market to develop and select the clothes to be shown. All size ranges in women's wear are included (except infants) together with some menswear.

This show accomplishes a number of important things for its sponsor. It promotes and publicizes the Milliken name and the trade names of its various fabrics and finishes. It encourages manufacturers to select Milliken fabrics for their lines to qualify for inclusion in the show. It thus assures Milliken of a distribution of its fabrics to a wide segment of the market.

3. The Professional Show to Analyze Trends

The professional fashion show is discussed here because it is related to the trade show. It is generally given at the beginning of a market season to analyze the fashion trends of the coming season by showing examples in a show presentation.

A prime example of the professional fashion show is those given by The Fashion Group of New York, and also by its Regional Groups in other cities and countries. These are essentially planned to disseminate fashion-trend information to members and their guests, most of whom are also in the profession.

Another example is the shows given by New York buying offices for their member stores at the beginning of a season to crystallize the major trends before the merchandising executives go into the market to buy. Some of these are elaborately done in a hotel ballroom, while others are informal presentations in a conference room of the buying office.

Similar shows are given by various fashion and merchandising consultants for their client stores for the same reason.

4. The Magazine Show

There are several occasions on which a magazine holds a fashion show. The fashion and service magazines rarely give shows for consumers, although they may participate in a consumer show given by a store.

Shows given by publications are generally trade shows for some segment of the fashion industry. It may be to delineate a coming season's fashions for store buyers, such as *Seventeen*'s annual Fall Trends

A scene from "The Young Expressionists" fashion show given by *Seventeen* Magazine for retail store executives in the Waldorf-Astoria. The same garment is worn by twelve models for impact.

The same scene interpreted by The Broadway of Los Angeles in their Hollywood Bowl fashion show for teens. Courtesy of Broadway Department Stores.

Show for store executives. This is given in June when buyers are in the market purchasing back-to-school fashions. It presents to them the magazine's beliefs about the seasonal fashion trends by showing a cross-section of fashions to be featured in the August and September issues. The clothes are grouped by fashion themes and are staged with appropriate promotional ideas. The magazine is interested in stimulating stores to stock the fashions so that readers can find them locally. The trade and daily press are also invited to this production, resulting in publicity as a secondary advantage.

Mademoiselle similarly produces a college fashion show for retailers and press. The clothes for this June presentation are a preview of the August college issue. *Bride's* is host at a black-tie dinner for retailers and press, twice a year, to show new wedding fashions.

THE SHOW TO TRAIN STORE PERSONNEL

At the beginning of a new season, stores with fashion reputations train their selling personnel in the major new fashions and "looks."

This is accomplished by means of a fashion show, which the store's fashion coordinator or owner (in the case of a smaller shop) stages. In order to whet the interest of those who are responsible for the selling success of the new fashions, the show is made as beautiful and dramatic as possible. Clothes from stock, completely accessorized, are grouped by major fashion themes — silhouettes, colors, fabrics, ideas, or whatever the key stories of the season are. The fashion coordinator explains to this professional audience the major fashion selling points and why the store is stocking these clothes.

Since many stores now have a number of branches, the fashion coordinator may package the show (complete with clothes, accessories, and models) and run a caravan to each branch.

Stores that seasonally stage a big consumer fashion extravaganza may invite the selling staff to attend the dress rehearsal as their training show. This has two advantages: (1) it is more economical than a separate show, and (2) it enables the personnel to know beforehand exactly what the customers will see so that they are prepared for calls for the merchandise.

Many stores consider the training show to be even more important than shows for customers. If the salespeople don't know the complete fashion story and aren't enthusiastic about the merchandise, the showing of the merchandise to customers will not accomplish much. For example, one store turned its dining room into a 1920s environment to put across new fashions inspired by that period. Stage settings recreated the inside of a speakeasy, while a jazz pianist added to the mood. Slides of personalities of the era made it all the more real. After salespeople, buyers, and advertising and display personnel saw the show, complete sales manuals were distributed.

THE SHOW TO RELEASE NEWS TO THE PRESS

Publicity through the press can spread the fashion message far and wide — and very fast. The press today includes not only newspapers and magazines but also radio, television, and the wire services that can literally flash a message around the world in a matter of moments. Thus the sun almost never sets on press shows.

The couture and made-to-order departments of stores show to the press before opening to customers. Stores give press shows to introduce new designers to the public, to open new departments, and to launch promotions such as a French Fortnight or an Irish Festival. Manufacturers invite the press for previews of their lines.

The snapper of the press show is that the merchandise or the idea must be new. The press is in business to disseminate news. Thus a press show cannot be given even a day after the customers have seen the merchandise. On the contrary, the purpose of publicity from the store's standpoint is to let customers know about the event via the press beforehand and to interest them in coming to see for themselves.

At a press showing, it is customary to distribute pertinent information in the form of press "releases" and appropriate glossy pictures, although some reporters will bring their own photographers to take exclusive pictures (or ask the show sponsor to provide exclusives). Releases are not usually run by the press as written, but are used as reference for accurate facts and figures when writing the stories. (Chapter 12 covers the specifics of providing this material.)

THE SHOW TO TRAIN FASHION AND DESIGN STUDENTS

As a part of their training, students in merchandising, retailing, and design schools plan and produce fashion shows as a part of their training for careers in these fields.

The fashion-merchandising schools generally borrow clothes from a friendly store for their shows. Credit is given to the store in a program

Model showing a gown by an award-winning student of Parsons School of Design, against screens bearing the signatures of noted Parsons graduates.

or in the commentary. In design schools, students create the fashions themselves. Parsons School of Design students present an annual show at a black-tie dinner in a New York hotel. On this same occasion awards are presented to outstanding students by some of the noted designer graduates of Parsons. Design students of the Fashion Institute of Technology stage a professional show in the school's auditorium, while Pratt Institute shows its students' designs at a hotel show.

Responsibilities for all phases of the show are divided among the students so they may have the total experience of planning, staging, selecting, modeling, and producing the show. This show is often the climax of graduation festivities and demonstrates what the students have learned.

THE SHOW FOR THE PRESENTATION OF AWARDS

A big fashion show often accompanies the presentation of awards or provides the entertainment at such an event. A glamorous show is expected in this case.

The most famous awards in the fashion industry are the Coty American Fashion Critics' Awards to American designers. The winners are chosen each year by a jury composed of the New York editors of magazines, newspapers, wire services, radio, and television who regularly cover and report on American fashions. The trophies are awarded at a fashion showing of designs by past and present winners, before a black-tie audience of leaders in the fashion industry and special guests. Under the supervision of Eleanor Lambert, the production is traditionally one of the most dramatic and beautiful, showing the finest of American fashion design.

Neiman-Marcus of Dallas, Texas, bestows annual awards in recognition of outstanding fashion leadership at a fashion spectacular in Dallas. Special guests fly in from all over the world to join an audience of local customers and dignitaries. The Neiman-Marcus Awards help the store to retain a high fashion image, bring untold publicity, and build good will among both designers and the public.

The Sunday Times of London initiated International Fashion Awards in 1963 at a gala evening fashion show in the Hilton Hotel in London. With ambassadors from winners' countries among the guests, the Duchess of Buccleuch and Queensbury made the presentations to fashion designers (and one hairdresser) from France, Italy, the United States, and England. Ernestine Carter, fashion editor, conceived the awards and the show to project fashion as part of the cultural scene. Michael Whittaker of London staged a fast-paced production with no

Silhouetted for drama, Geoffrey Beene's black evening fashions are modeled at the Coty American Fashion Critics' Awards presentations in the Metropolitan Museum of Art, 1964. Courtesy of Coty.

spoken commentary. After Mary Quant, he was one of the first to dare to let the fashions speak for themselves.

THE SHOW FOR PURE ENTERTAINMENT

Many organizations (usually women's) regard a fashion show as prime entertainment. For various functions such as an annual luncheon or card party, a fund-raising affair, or a big charity benefit, the entertainment committee often decides to produce a fashion show. In many cases, the committee has no idea of the task it is undertaking.

The first problem is where to get the clothes. If the organization is important enough, a shop or store may be willing to cooperate. However, many stores have strict policies against giving shows outside of the store because of the wear and tear on the clothes, the losses, and the thefts. Also a store's primary aim in any fashion show is to sell merchandise. Therefore, the showing of clothes outside the store isn't conducive to an immediate response on the part of the audience.

Michael Whittaker, left, directs a dress rehearsal of the International Fashion Awards show given by *The Sunday Times* of London, 1965. Reproduced by permission of *The Sunday Times,* London. Copyright, Thomson Newspapers.

An elegant setting is designed by Michael Whittaker, seen directing a dress rehearsal, for a fashion presentation for Her Royal Highness the Duchess of Gloucester, to benefit the Red Cross Charity, at Celanese House in London. Copyright, E. R. Waters.

Some stores have a policy of limiting their participation in outside shows to a certain number or to one or two specific charity or civic shows a year. They may absorb all expenses as their contribution, or they may require some token on the part of the organization. One store asks that the music be provided — but with its approval. Several ask flat fees of around $200 to $500 to cover models and other costs. One store in a major convention city charges from $500 to $1000 for a convention show but charges nothing when it agrees to do a civic or charity event. The merchants' associations in some cities have established rules for all stores. The members of one association have agreed that all stores will make a token charge of $15 for any organization show except for a recognized charity. The retailers in another city have a mutual agreement that the sponsoring organization must make a contribution toward the costs of a store show, usually the ballroom rental.

Some stores will produce special shows in the store for women's clubs. For example, B. Altman of New York has attractive club rooms in its branch stores that local organizations may use free. Since the store agrees to produce a certain number of shows each year in these rooms, the organizations book a year or more in advance for this privilege.

The couture shows given as part of the "April in Paris" balls in New York for many years are examples of fashion as entertainment. This ball always benefits a French cause. Consequently, some member of the French or American couture is always willing to lend his collection each year to provide a luxurious show.

The fashion industry in New York has a beautiful pageant of fashion each year as the feature of its "Party of the Year" benefit for the Costume Institute of the Metropolitan Museum. On this occasion, the Museum opens its doors to the industry for a black-tie party that starts with a reception around the pool and continues with a catered dinner at tables set up in the Great Hall. Following dinner, priceless costumes from the Museum's collection are modeled by fashion celebrities on a center platform. A theme is followed for the whole party and carried through in the costumes shown. At one affair, for example, a peasant theme was chosen for the decorations, while the most magnificent peasant costumes from all over the world comprised the show.

Fashion Shows as Television Entertainment

Although fashion shows have not yet become major television entertainment, they are given regularly in some form. Most are confined to local stations because of the tremendous production and time costs involved. Also, this kind of show on prime time would not appeal to the widest possible audience. Male viewers might defect in spite of the attractive models.

Network fashion shows are generally short segments on talk shows or variety shows, or an occasional news flash. Shows such as "Merv Griffin," "Mike Douglas," "Today," and "Tonight" add variety with these capsule fashion shows. Naturally, they prefer a newsworthy idea: a preview of Paris imports or a review of a new talked-about fashion. The purpose of the fashion show is pure entertainment, but those providing the fashions are eager for nationwide publicity and usually underwrite all expenses of the production including the substantial models' fees.

One big, coast-to-coast television show is the annual Pageant produced by American Wool Council at San Angelo, Texas (a wool center) on the occasion of the selection and crowning of Miss Wool of America. The college-girl contestants model wool fashions from the best American designers in an elaborately staged show that stars celebrities from the entertainment world. The show is beamed more toward obtaining publicity than selling merchandise. Wool, per se, is publicized in fashions by noted designers.

Network-production shows are frequently taped beforehand, which allows for more movement and variety in backgrounds, as well as unusual effects. The small segments in the talk shows are live (although the whole show itself may be taped), which limits the action but requires only the simplest setting.

Filmed Shows

The new-again fashion show on film is mentioned here, since it is similar to a taped television show. This show, like television, has entertainment as its reason for being, even though the sponsor is selling the fashions. Although growing in interest, the fashion film has been limited because of the costs involved and because of the time lag between filming and releasing which means that the fashions must be designed ahead.

4

Planning a Compatible Show and Audience

Because women and girls like fashion shows, there is a never-ending supply of audiences. However, a show is so costly in time, effort, and expense that it should be designed to draw maximum attendance by the right kind of audience. A show that draws guests who are not potential customers for the merchandise is wasteful. Empty seats are wasteful, too, and are depressing to everyone (the staff and the audience).

To succeed at producing the most exciting event possible, the show and audience must be compatible in every way. The preceding chapter discussed in detail the types of fashion shows and the audiences that they aim to attract. However, it takes more than luck to make the show and the audience compatible. These two requisites (discussed below) must be fulfilled:

1. A potential audience must really exist within the geographical area from which the show is likely to draw, at the time the show is given.
2. The show and the audience must fit each other with respect to the merchandise, the timing, the prices, the commentary, and the presentation.

ARE THEY OUT THERE

Before considering anything else about the potential compatibility of your show and audience, be sure there are enough persons out there to make the show pay off. If not, plan another type of show that will bring in more people, or alter your show plans to bring expense and effort into line with the number who can be reached.

A store in a wealthy, exclusive neighborhood of older persons might not reach enough teens or enough business women. On the other hand, it might reach an abundance of women who wear high-fashion clothes.

Another example is the "Please Do Touch The Merchandise" fashion shows for blind teen-age girls that *Seventeen* planned in 1967-1968 in cooperation with a group of stores across the country. Since very special arrangements were necessary for handling the audience and staging the show, these events had to be confined to cities where there were schools for the blind with enough girls in the age group to make up an audience.

THE PERFECT FIT

After you have measured the size of the potential attendance at a particular show and are satisfied, you must follow through with plans that will interest the selected group and draw the largest possible number.

Tell a Clear Story

The first step toward attracting a good audience is to know clearly what you are trying to sell and the fashion story that you are trying to tell.

In a retail store it is best to single out one classification of merchandise, or one occasion for which different kinds of merchandise may be worn, instead of presenting a mixed bag. This draws a homogeneous audience and offers the best sales potential. A bridal show draws prospective brides. A maternity show attracts mothers-to-be. A college show brings in young people who are planning to enter college. Naturally there are always some who come for the show, no matter what it is, but the majority who attend are likely to be interested in buying the merchandise.

On the other hand, a fashion show of mixed merchandise is likely to draw the wrong audience, or none at all, because the customer is confused about what is to be shown. For example, a general "back-to-school" fashion show, which some stores are tempted to give in the fall, might span an audience that ranges from first-graders to college seniors. This makes it extremely difficult to bring off a successful show because the presentation itself cannot be interesting to all, and because the different age groups don't even want to be in the same room together. The result may be a preponderance of one group or simply overall poor attendance.

It is much better to plan smaller shows for specific target audiences. Each group will then know that the clothes, the presentation, the entertainment, and the audience are for it alone.

In a restaurant at lunchtime the models are likely to perform to a mixture of business girls and housewives, while at teatime the audience

The pants fashion is singled out by Abraham & Straus and presented on wheels in Prospect Park, Brooklyn. Special entertainment is provided by a group of performing unicyclists, and the commentator sits astride a bicycle.

A bicycle-built-for-two wheels a team of models around the course at the Abraham & Straus "The Big Wheels of Fall" pants show in Prospect Park.

Teens are the enthusiastic target of Du Pont's "Teen Pop Concert" fashion show at May-D & F, Denver.

would tend to be all housewives. Thus a good selection of fashions for informal modeling on these occasions mixes street and dressy clothes for younger women and matrons.

If the show is for entertainment, dramatic fashions and showpieces make the most exciting presentation because the entertainment value is the criterion. Good gimmicky clothes can also be amusing.

When showing to the press, news value is the yardstick for selecting the fashions. The show might present a new season's new fashions (no carryovers), a new designer, or one new fashion idea. An example of a new idea is the pants fashion for women that swept the country in the fall of 1968. Many all-pants shows were given to exemplify the many types of pants and the varied occasions for which they could be worn.

The Format Must Fit

The way in which a fashion show is packaged must be appropriate for those who will attend. For instance:

- A show for consumers can have as much entertainment as you wish, commensurate with the amount of time you have for the show and with the type of audience — as long as the clothes emerge as the stars.

- If business women are your audience at a lunchtime show, make the format short and punchy, since their time is limited. (A box lunch at a nominal price is an added service to this audience.) If the show is after working hours, there is more leeway in the presentation. Make it light and gay, since the audience is likely to be tired and want to relax.

- A high-fashion couture show should have a sophisticated presentation. Since the clothes themselves have high interest value, the entertainment can be kept to a minimum. The ideal audience at this kind of show is women who are likely to buy the clothes. Thus a part of their entertainment is seeing other guests and being seen.

- When the press attends a fashion show, it is one of their daily assignments among many others. A story must be written or telephoned in afterward. For these reasons, entertainment can be cut to a minimum. Any newsworthy background or way of showing the clothes is welcome as long as it doesn't get in the way of the story The news among the merchandise itself must be clearly apparent.

- A training show for employees can be simply handled so that the big selling points emerge clearly. Also, time and budget are always limited. The essentials are strong fashion groupings, good models, total accessorizing. However, some stores, which realize the importance of training, go all out with elaborate shows.

- If the audience is present at a benefit or party to have a good time and the show is for the purpose of entertaining, the fashions may become subordinate and a real show may take over. A television show must always have a strong entertainment value, even if the primary purpose is to sell merchandise. Celebrities modeling or entertaining are an excellent addition to this type of show.

- For an awards presentation, the show should have the finest and most sophisticated presentation. It can be amusing, of course, at the same time. However, the giving of a serious award deserves elegance and beauty as a setting.

- Any trade show, whether given by a manufacturer to present his line or a big trade association to publicize merchandise of its members, demands professional presentation. The reasons behind the merchandise must be made apparent in an interesting way. Buyers, like press, are busy and can't afford to sit through nonpertinent entertainment. However, any dramatization of the merchandise or

Fashions by noted designers are presented in a setting of elegance by Filene's French Shops in Boston. As a prelude to this evening scene, six projectors illuminated the ceiling with films of fireworks from the Fête de Nuit at Versailles.

any new ideas in presentation are welcome if they give the buyer suggestions for selling it to his customers when the time comes. In a showroom, this can take the form of decor, programs, promotion kits, and other supporting material, rather than being incorporated in the showing itself.

Some trade shows are given partly for public relations and entertainment, as well as to sell. In this case, the show and entertainment must be good and professional. It is best to have it outside of working hours when the audience feels more relaxed about spending extra time for the event. Examples are the Milliken Breakfast Show with breakfast at 7 A.M. and final curtain at 9 A.M., and the semiannual dinner and fashion show given after the workday by Millinery Institute.

The Price Must be Right

Any fashion show for the purpose of directly selling merchandise to anyone must emphasize merchandise at prices that the audience is most likely to be able to pay. Add a sprinkling at a slightly higher price as the frosting on the cake.

This rule works the other way too. If you have specific merchandise to show, be sure to invite an audience whose purses fit the prices of the fashions. A high-fashion, high-priced show requires an invitation audience of persons who normally buy and wear this type of clothes. A newspaper ad, inviting the general public, is wasteful and pointless.

A show for business girls features prices that are in line with local salaries. An event for teens takes into consideration that they like lots of clothes at moderate prices.

Talk to the Audience

If a script or commentary is used in a show, make its style compatible with the audience. It is obvious that you would not talk in the same way to teens, men, brides, and matrons.

THE PROPER SEASONING

Stores and manufacturers are aware that their fashion shows must be timed by the selling seasons.

Manufacturers show their lines or collections during "market" periods when retail buyers are making purchases for an upcoming season. Dates vary in different markets and from year to year. In New York, the largest ready-to-wear market, spring fashions are shown in October and November; summer fashions in February; fall-winter fashions in April, May, and June; and holiday fashions in September.

Stores should give their shows at the beginning of a consumer selling season when stocks are fresh, new, and at their peak. This means spring shows in February and March; summer shows any time after Easter; back-to-school and college shows at the end of July or during August; fall-winter fashions in September; and holiday fashions in October and November.

Organizations that ask stores to provide fashions for shows can have more exciting presentations if they follow this same timing. During the off months (for instance, January when reductions are in order) the stores are unable to put together a good show. The stocks are broken and the fashion stories have lost impact and excitement by the end of the season.

Press shows are in order when the fashion story is red hot: before manufacturers show to retailers so that the news may be broken in the trade press (this is too early for the daily press), or before stores show to customers so that stories may break in the daily press. Since magazine editors plan several months in advance, they frequently must work with the designers before the press preview, but they like to attend the press shows to see the finished collection in order to confirm their own thinking.

For some years, special fashion Press Weeks have been given in New York, Los Angeles, and Dallas for the daily working press. These are sponsored by manufacturers who hold special spring and fall showings after the retailers have covered these markets, but before the fashions are in the stores. This gives women's-page and fashion editors a scoop on the fashion news.

When scheduling shows, even days and hours have to be considered. These must coincide with times when the prospective audience is available. For example, teens can attend only on Saturdays or after school, except in summer when they may be away at camp. After school may be inconvenient for students because they have extracurricular activities and lessons to prepare. Also it may mean being out after dark, to which many parents object.

Shows for business women have to be given outside of office hours, which means at lunchtime or after work on an evening when the store is open. Whether they will attend a show on Saturday depends on local geography. If going downtown means a long trip, the chances are that there would be no audience. Suburban stores are likely to fare better.

"The Out of Sight Flight," a unique teen fashion show sponsored by Titche's of Dallas at the American Airlines hanger. Staged in August when teens have the time to travel to a suburban locale.

Mothers are better able to attend shows when children are in school. This eliminates afternoon shows.

Whatever your target audience group is, measure it against the times when it is likely to be free and available. Then schedule the show accordingly.

5

Selecting the Place for the Show

Fashion shows have been given on ships, in planes, in front of the New York Public Library on Fifth Avenue, in the Hollywood Bowl, and almost anywhere that you can imagine. However, the difficulties presented by some places are so numerous that it's wiser to look for a different locale rather than attempt to overcome the problems. If you ignore the handicaps, you will soon run into trouble and may have a disaster on your hands. The wise producer will look for the most compatible place possible to make it easier on the nerves and to assure a successful show.

In some instances, the place where the fashion show is held is predetermined by the circumstances. In that event, all plans for the show must relate to the circumstances that exist. This chapter deals with selecting a place that will satisfy the maximum number of requirements, but it should also be used as a check in overcoming handicaps that are inherent in the locale to which you are confined.

THE ROOM AND THE AUDIENCE MUST FIT

The number of persons who will attend the show must fit comfortably into the room where it will be held. Like a pair of gloves, it is better to have a good, snug fit (with even a few standees) than to have empty seats or unused space. A capacity audience is stimulating to models, musicians, and other participants. To look out on empty seats is to feel that nobody came to the party. This makes it difficult for the cast to sparkle and give their best.

If you are producing a recurrent show or a customer show for a store, estimate (from past experience) what the response will be, based on the promotional efforts, and how much or how little promotion you must do to fill the number of available seats.

The stage of the mammoth Hollywood Bowl lends drama in itself to a young show sponsored by The Broadway on a warm August evening. Courtesy of Broadway Department Stores.

The courtyard of the Alhambra in Granada, Spain, provides a naturally glamorous setting for an Amcel-Europe evening fashion show. Director Michael Whittaker instructs the models at a morning rehearsal.

On one occasion an ambitious store went all out in publicizing an evening show, while the only auditorium available in the town was a small ballroom with a seating capacity of around 300. At least twice that many guests turned up. The pianist fled in dismay when standees almost smothered her, leaving the show with no music at all. Half of the guests had to turn around and go home, not only disappointed but also annoyed with the host store. To avoid such an unfortunate situation, this store would have been well advised to soft-pedal the promotion and possibly have an invitation audience, or to schedule two shows to satisfy the demand. (Incidentally, this is a good reason for issuing tickets, as discussed in Chapter 12.)

There are two other essential considerations when booking a room for a fashion show.

1. There may be fire laws governing the number of persons who may occupy a room, in which case the number is usually posted. Naturally, these laws must be observed when planning a show.
2. Check whether there are adequate entrances and exits so that no bottlenecks occur in getting the audience in and out of the room. Exits are generally required to be lighted and kept free.

THE ROOM CAN ADD GLAMOUR TO THE SHOW

If you have a free hand in choosing a place to hold a fashion show, consider finding one that ties in with the theme or that adds glamour or interest to the show. A new place helps to draw an audience.

The prestigious Coty Fashion Critics' Awards show, which had been held for many years at the Metropolitan Museum of Art in New York, now takes place in the Alice Tully Hall at Lincoln Center. These surroundings add dignity and prestige, and provide appropriate settings.

When the new fiber Trevira was introduced in 1968, the company chose the famous Parke-Bernet Galleries on Madison Avenue in New York (where paintings and art objects are often sold for over a million dollars) to give prestige to their introductory show.

A theater is a good setting for a fashion show staged as a musical. (However, dressing room space must be checked carefully for adequacy and positioning.) A hotel ballroom may add a desired element of elegance to one type of show, although it may be too elegant for another type such as a teen show.

All kinds of unusual places have been chosen for big teen shows that fill the requirements of informality, space, and variety. Some smashing shows have been staged in airplane hangers where airlines or airports

Wednesday's in New York becomes the compatible setting for an intimate sportswear show given by Du Pont for the press and retail buyers.

have been willing to cooperate, such as Titche's show in American Airlines' hanger at Love Field in Dallas. The Broadway of Los Angeles has taken over the Hollywood Bowl for their young shows, while Lamson's of Toledo staged probably the most unique show of all on a strip of highway.

Since members of the fashion press are overburdened with invitations to showings, they welcome a new and novel setting. However, they prefer not to have to travel to a remote spot because they are on assignment. If a show is given out of town or anywhere that requires traveling a distance, buses are appreciated. Be sure that there are return buses at frequent intervals so that no one is stranded for hours. The press is skilled at getting a story quickly.

EVERYONE WANTS TO SEE THE SHOW

There's nothing more frustrating than attending a show that you cannot see! There are several obstructions to sight that may interfere with the audience's enjoyment of the show. Be on guard and check out these possibilities:

An unusual spot for a fashion show is the American Airlines hanger at Love Field in Dallas, where Titche's staged a teen show. It required a lot of scrubbing to ready the hanger.

One of the most original locales of any fashion show is an unopened new strip of Highway 475 near Toledo, Ohio, where Lamson's staged "Alive on 475" for local girls and boys.

The rock band tunes up near the scaffolding erected in the middle of Highway 475 in preparation for Lamson's "Alive on 475" show.

Models rehearse on the scaffolding that forms the stage setting for Lamson's "Alive 475" teen fashion show on Highway 475 near Toledo.

1. *Posts and pillars.* There may be so many big ones that a large part of the audience would have little or no visibility. Choose another place.

2. *Stage and curtains.* The stage may be located in the room or the front curtains may be hung so that guests seated on the sides near the front are completely out of the sight line. In this event, do not seat guests in these areas, or do not use the back of the stage for action or models' entry. If you can spare the space, the first choice is preferable.

3. *Elevation.* The floor of the room may be level so that it is difficult to see except in the front. The solution is to be sure the stage and runway are high enough. Platforms on the stage may be used to build height. Also, be sure that the runway is long enough so that everyone has a good view, even if they can't see the stage well.

4. *Balconies.* Sometimes guests seated in a large balcony are unable to see the front of the stage or a runway if these extend too far into the room. Also the view from a hotel-ballroom tier may be obstructed. When a new ballroom was built at a cost of several million dollars in the old Astor Hotel in New York in the early 1960s, the crystal chandeliers were so big and so numerous that it was impossible to see the stage from the tier. All of the chandeliers had to be raised. So check all parts of a balcony, box, or tier to be sure that visibility is good. Otherwise, don't seat guests there.

HOW TO FIND THE BEST FASHION SHOW SETTING

To find the most interesting and workable setting for a fashion show, use your imagination and your friends. Think of all of the local places that are possible, and also of those you may think impossible. Ask any of your friends who attend parties and functions for suggestions. Sometimes you can book a private club through a generous friend, or because your own organization is a prestigious one that the club is proud to have.

You can obtain a great deal of pertinent information over the telephone about any place you are interested in. If it sounds at all possible, make an appointment to look over the facilities and discuss your needs with the person in charge.

As a starting point, here is a list of some possible locales for a fashion show:

Store auditorium.
Store tearoom, restaurant, club room, employee cafeteria, an open selling floor.

The exhibit buildings at HemisFair in San Antonio, Texas, form a natural background and arena for Joske's fashion show staged in the open air.

Club or hotel dining room, meeting room, ballroom, poolside.
Auditoriums — civic, school, club, church, lodge.
Gymnasiums (be sure that the dressing rooms are clean).
Parking lots or parking roofs (be sure that they are clean).
Theater or movie houses.
Novelty spots — zoo, tent in a park, street or square, opera house, concert hall, museum, gallery, sports arena, fair grounds.

PLEASE BE SEATED

Since an audience is more likely to be attentive if it is comfortably seated, try to have enough seats. A slight overflow of standees is permissible if there is a place for them to stand without obstructing the view of others. This even has a good psychological effect.

Whether to seat concert-fashion with rows of chairs or at tables depends on the kind of show. If food is served, it is best to have tables unless service is in another room. It is quite usual and successful to serve guests in an adjoining room from a buffet or even at a seated collation, either before or after the show. In this case, concert seating is generally used for the show.

If a show is given in a tearoom or restaurant, the management may not want to remove tables and chairs, even if no food is being served. This is acceptable, since it gives guests a place to put programs and handbags.

When planning seating, consider whether to assign specific seats or tables to the guests, or whether to let them sit where they wish.

HOW TO CHECK THE FACILITIES

There are a number of facilities that are essential to running a smooth fashion show. Because the show is usually given only once (or, at most, several times), you must work within the set-up of the place you choose. A Broadway show, which always anticipates a long run, spends the money necessary to provide the facilities it needs. You can't afford this for a fashion show.

"Fashions on Ice," a show to publicize the United Hospital Fund, takes place at the Rockefeller Center Skating Rink in New York, sponsored by Singer. The locale inspires the theme and provides the setting. Courtesy of The Singer Company.

All of the models in the Singer "Fashions on Ice" show to publicize the United Hospital Fund must at least be able to stand up on skates. Courtesy of The Singer Company.

Check the Union Status

The first detail to check is the union status of any hotel, club, or other building where you contemplate having a show. Ask whether musicians, electrical experts, or any other specialists involved must be union members. If a very tight union situation exists, it may be well to consider another place. Never take a chance on trying to use nonunion people in a solidly union house. You might find not only your show shut down but a whole building at a standstill. If any nonunion workers are needed for any special reason in a union house, be prepared to pay standbys.

Check the Dressing Room

The very nature of the fashion show means lots of clothes and accessories, and a sizable complement of models and dressers. The first requirement of the dressing room is that it be large enough for all of the models and workers to be comfortable and for racks of clothes and tables of accessories to be accessible. In addition, you may need space for props, pressers with their ironing boards, hairdressers, makeup artists, and even an alteration woman for last-minute stitches or repairs. Also, models are notoriously thirsty and hungry, so you may need a table for water, coffee, or sandwiches.

There is no scientific way of figuring how much space is needed per model because each show varies. All of the above-mentioned possibilities must be considered, and your own space requirement must be arrived at.

The lighting must be adequate for models to be able to dress carefully and use makeup skillfully.

Because quick changes invariably occur in a show, and because models tend to get lost, the dressing room must be near the stage or run-

A young model takes off with an adult at the Singer "Fashions on Ice" show on the Rockefeller Center Skating Rink in New York. Courtesy of The Singer Company.

way—adjacent if possible. Dressing rooms upstairs or downstairs (the usual layout in a regular theater) are a serious handicap. Since they require more time for models to make the trip, they necessitate more models. They also require additional show staff to man stairways and corridors. Another handicap is the lack of communication between the dressing rooms and the stage.

Cleanliness is essential in a dressing room because expensive merchandise can be ruined and made unsalable if it is soiled in a dirty room. A bridal show is a particularly touchy one where cleanliness is involved because of the perishability of the clothes and colors.

Adequate rest rooms must be available to models and show staff. These should be checked for cleanliness because models will use them while wearing show clothes (you simply can't prevent it).

Check Stage or Platform and Runway

If the room you select has a stage, examine the stage to be sure that the size is right for your show—not too big, not too small. If everything else is desirable, but the stage is not quite the right size, consider altering the show to fit the stage.

The ideal height of the stage is 36 inches from the floor. Since this is a little higher than a table, it enables seated guests to see well. If the stage has an "apron" (extension) out into the room, you have more space for the show and visibility is better (except, possibly from a balcony).

You may have to rent or build a platform if there is no stage. Private clubs and country clubs, for example, have few or no fashion show-facilities. When providing your own platform, keep in mind:

- The platform should be stage height—36 inches.
- It should be steady so that models are not nervous and will not fall.
- Plan a setting or background that does not require curtains.
- Consider a theater-in-the-round set-up with the platform in the center of the room.
- You will probably need one or two sets of steps leading to the platform. Be sure these are steady and will not tip over. Many models have been injured and embarrassed by falls from unsteady steps.
- Remember that the platform will need to be covered. Carpeting is preferable. The outdoor or kitchen carpeting can be used satisfactorily and is much less expensive than a regular carpeting. A solid color is best—one that ties in with the color scheme—or a neutral tone. Felted fabrics are not good for covering a platform, since the models' heels quickly wear through. (Cover the platform after re-

To celebrate the opening of a new distribution center in Atlanta, Penney's erects scaffolding and platforms to tie in with the building interior. Courtesy of J. C. Penney Company.

hearsals if possible.) If there is to be dancing in the show, check with the dancers. They may need a wooden or other special flooring. Rental dance floors are available—look for suppliers under "Dance Floors—Portable—Renting" in the classified section of the telephone directory.

The runway should be a standard 36 inches high and 36 inches wide, or it may be wider for special productions. Brides and dogs need more space! One fashion coordinator rented a big English sheep dog to model with fun furs. When the human model pivoted, the obedient animal tried to follow the lead, but the 36-inch runway proved too narrow. As he turned sideways, his front feet slipped off one side, while his hind legs slipped off the other, and he sprawled flat.

Many hotels keep sections of runway in these specifications for the purpose of forming platforms or runways. Check to see what is available to you. If you must provide your own, and if you do shows regularly in such places, it is worthwhile to have your own portable runway sections constructed and carpeting provided. Good dimensions for such sections are:

36 inches high
36 to 40 inches wide
6 to 8 feet long

Add some portable sections of strip lights to edge the runway, and a professional look will be achieved. You will also need one or two sets of steady steps that fit onto the runway.

Covering a runway is the same as covering a platform (as described above). Hotels seem to like carpeting with big, unattractive patterns. So ask to see the material with which they usually cover their runways. If you don't like it (and you probably won't), provide your own. The indoor-outdoor carpetings are good and are less expensive. If you construct your own runway, it may be made with a covering of vinyl tiles that look nice and are easy to clean after each use. The runway also requires a "skirt" to cover the sides. Here again, that provided may be unattractive, so check. A duvetyn or any other fabric is appropriate.

The length of the runway depends on the size and shape of the room. In a room that is fairly square in shape, the runway should come to the center of the room. If the room is long and narrow, bring it two-thirds to three-quarters of the length of the room

Check Lighting and Stage Rigging

The lighting of the room itself is not terribly important, as long as the guests can find their seats without injury. Naturally, attractive "mood" lighting adds to any event, such as dimmed lights or any special architectural lighting that is a part of the room.

The lighting of the stage and runway is of the utmost importance, as are the facilities for proper placement of lighting units. The clothes in a fashion show must be well lighted so that the audience can readily see details, colors, textures, and accessories. It is also important that the models' hair styles are visible, and the makeup colors not distorted. These are part of the total fashion look.

Rarely are the normal lights in a room adequate for lighting a show. The models need to be spotlighted. In addition to aiding visibility, this adds to the drama of the show. Some hotels have a few spotlights and can provide operators (there is an extra charge for both lights and operators). However, check out whether these lights are sufficient for your staging. If you must rent equipment, look for suppliers under "Theatrical Equipment and Supplies" in the yellow pages of the telephone book.

Footlights on stage and runway, in addition to spots, add greatly to the lighting and excitement of the show. Whether there are enough electrical outlets, and whether the normal power lines can take extra lighting equipment must also be ascertained. No show can survive a blown fuse.

If the show is to take place in a theater or auditorium with a well equipped stage, footlights and spots are usually an integral part of the setup.

For a major show, it is desirable to employ a lighting expert who can prescribe what is needed, who is in a position to provide or rent the equipment, and who will supply and supervise the operating crew.

Closely related to the lighting, in staging a show, is the rigging equipment available on a stage. This means the facitities for installing sets and hanging curtains or other scenery. Be sure that any setting planned can be handled with the equipment available. It is almost too elementary to mention, but height, width, and depth of stage must be measured before planning any staging.

Check the PA System

In show parlance, the "PA" is the public address system. Does your show locale have the facilities you need, or must you provide them? Not only does the commentator need a good microphone (neck mike, standing mike, or one fixed to the podium — don't expect the commentator to hold the mike and handle a script or cards), but performers also may need PA equipment.

Someone should be on hand during the show to make sure that the sound is properly adjusted at all times for the voices, and to keep it functioning. At one of the magnificent "Party of the Year" pageants, the microphone broke down early in the show and was never put back in operation. Modeling celebrities such as Carol Channing crossed the runway without introduction, and precious costumes were shown without any explanation of the source. The embarrassed commentator was herself a celebrity.

The Commentator's Needs

In addition to a good microphone of the type that the commentator prefers, she is more comfortable if a podium is provided. (Most commentators are women because of their fashion knowledge, but men make excellent commentators and the specifications apply to them too.) If she is nervous, the podium gives her something to hold onto. More important, it gives her a place to put her script or cards and any special notes. It provides a place for a glass of water and a cache for her handbag or eyeglasses.

The podium must be equipped with a workable light (check it just before show time). More than one commentator has walked out to a dark podium with no means of seeing her notes and has had to ad lib every time the lights went down.

If two persons are to do a co-commentary, two microphones should be provided. Nothing looks more awkward than two persons passing a mike back and forth during an entire show. It is worse, still, to have two commentators taking turns at going to the mike and backing away.

The Needs of the Audience

Remember these requirements for the comfort of the audience:

1. *Adequate rest rooms in an accessible location.* If the place you choose is one that is regularly used for special events or parties, it is likely that you will have no problems. However, if you select an unusual spot, there may be no facilities at all. Consider carefully whether you believe it is necessary to rent portable rest rooms (yes, they do exist— look under "Toilets—Portable" in the yellow pages of the telephone book). One organization considered staging a big fashion show for 2000 persons on a New York pier. The complete lack of rest rooms and the necessity for bringing them in was a key factor in the decision not to use this otherwise interesting spot.

2. *A checkroom.* If there are only women in the audience, this can be eliminated as they usually prefer not to check coats. However, if the weather is bad, it is nicer to be able to check a wet wrap. If men are present, a checkroom is essential.

Whenever an unusual location is chosen for a show, it is wise to check whether there are any city ordinances that govern the number of persons who may be accommodated in the space, the exit, the restroom facilities, or any other details.

Facilities for Receiving Guests

You may need a special setup at the door for holding tickets, distributing seating lists, or taking tickets. Tables and chairs are normally available in almost any place that is accustomed to handling events. Ticket boxes may or may not be available. Just remember to check this when booking the place so that you know whether you must provide the needed equipment.

Reserve Rehearsal and Setting-Up Time

A problem often arises in connection with obtaining the room you have booked for the necessary rehearsals. The place may not be available because of other bookings—or you may be lucky enough to have carte blanche. There may even be a prohibitive rental fee because your rehearsal would prevent the use of the room for another event. Check this when making your reservation.

If the rehearsals cannot be held where the show will take place, it is necessary to find and reserve another place. There may be a dancing school with a large enough studio (look under "Dancing Instruction" in the yellow pages for the names of local dancing schools). You may be able to borrow a school or church auditorium, or a school gymnasium. In major cities, there are rehearsal halls for rent at reasonable fees. These are listed under "Rehearsal Studio Rental" or "Studio Rental" in the yellow pages.

In finding a place to rehearse, you need adequate space to mark off on the floor an approximation of the stage and runway that will actually be used. Use masking tape for this. You will also probably need to have a piano available.

If at all possible, a dress rehearsal should be arranged on the actual stage with sets and props. This might be done just before the show.

Another block of time that must be reserved is adequate time for setting up the stage, runway, dressing room, and guest area. For an elaborate show, this can take hours. Also, when the show is over, additional time is necessary to strike the sets and move everything out. Arrangements must be made for elevators needed, for hands to do this work, and possibly for trucking merchandise and props away.

SHOWS UNDER THE SKY

Nothing is lovelier than a pretty fashion show outdoors on a pleasant evening. If an open-air theater, drive-in movie, park, or other locale is available, it's difficult to resist the idea. However, an outdoor show presents many problems, even if under a tent. These are noted in Chapter 13, which discusses special kinds of shows. All requirements spelled out in this chapter must also be satisfied.

6

How to Plan and Organize the Show

To the uninitiated, a fashion show may give the impression of being an easy undertaking. However, like so many things that on the surface appear to be simple, there's a sizable staff behind the scene that spends hours and days (and, sometimes, months) planning and organizing every small detail. If the show looks smooth and effortless, it's because of good organization. As one wise fashion-show producer advised, "Have system rather than spontaneous combustion!"

THE FASHION SHOW STAFF

The size of the staff needed to produce a fashion show varies widely, depending on the size and extent of the show. The following functions must be performed for almost any show. Each function may require one or more persons, or one person may be responsible for several of them. Any one of these may be appropriately handled by a man or a woman; thus "he" and "she" are used here interchangeably.

Fashion Director

Someone who knows fashion well and who has good taste must take charge of this primary aspect of the show. Without a strong and exciting fashion story, there is no show. The fashion director:

Outlines the fashion sequences.
Selects the clothes.
Slots the clothes into the sequences.
Lines up the clothes in an interesting order.

Selects the models.
Fits the models.
Accessorizes the fashions.

Producer-Director

Responsibility for planning the entire presentation or production must be fixed with one person. Many times the fashion director takes on this extra task. Some store fashion directors have become almost as well known for their show talents as for their fashion knowledge.

To produce a spectacular, a trade show, a press show, or any of the special-occasion shows, a professional is desirable. Such an assignment takes a great deal of time and calls for a knowledge of good showmanship. There may be a local person who specializes in fashion shows. If not, consider the producer or director of a local repertory theater or little theater group, or a drama professor or teacher. On some occasions, models and college students have produced excellent shows.

Starting with the fashion director's list of fashion sequences, the producer plans the staging to set off the fashions. Unless the show is primarily for entertainment, he must give first thought to emphasizing the fashion story.

The producer also directs the rehearsals and takes charge during the show.

Set Designer

In a store the display manager generally doubles as the set and prop designer. The store may also be generous enough to offer his services whenever they lend clothes to an organization for a show.

The display manager of a store is sometimes able to work free-lance for outside organizations and may be employed for this purpose. These specialists are excellent for fashion shows because they are experienced in showing off fashions, and are schooled in getting the greatest effect for the least amount of money.

A display company frequently has a staff designer or has a designer on call. This person is a good one to use because he is familiar with construction and costs.

The set designer works with the fashion director and the producer in arriving at an attractive background for the show. The fashion director needs a foil for the clothes. The producer requires a setting that integrates with his action. This may be entrances, platforms, screens, and steps. The trend is toward simple, modern settings that provide a means for movement of the models. Watch television for trends and ideas in sets.

Script-Commentary Writer

Someone must put the show down on paper. This may be the fashion director or a copywriter, or the two together. No one knows the clothes better than the fashion director; therefore, she may prefer to do the writing.

If the show is straight modeling without any special staging, only a lineup needs to be written so that everyone working in the show knows the plan. The commentator may choose to ad lib or may write her descriptions.

A staged show demands a script, with cues, to be used by the entire staff during the rehearsals and the show. Every move expected of the participants is included in the script.

Music Director

The head musician may be made music director of the show. If you have only a pianist or an organist, this persons works with the staff as music authority. If a music group is booked, the leader becomes the music director.

The music director enters the picture as soon as he is chosen. He needs to know the general plans early enough to book the musicians that he will need. Since he is usually familiar with other local musicians, he can be very helpful in finding any special talent needed.

This key staff member should be given a complete script as soon as it is available so that he can plan the specific music. If there is no script for a straight show, he needs to know the fashion themes of the sequences and the number of models in each.

It is important that the music director attend rehearsals. It isn't necessary to assume the expense of having a whole group for any rehearsal except the final dress rehearsal with all the performers. Only a pianist is needed for regular rehearsals, and the music director may be able to fill this bill himself.

Choreographer

If there is to be any dancing or any special routines, a choreographer is needed to plan and rehearse the numbers. Professional choreographers are available in cities that have a theater or opera compnay. Dancing teachers can frequently fill this need very well.

Electrical Director or Electrician

Since lighting is an important key to a good show, an electrical director or at least a good electrician must be consulted. Hotels, clubs, auditoriums, and convention centers are likely to have head electricians who may suffice. They are frequently experienced in working on fashion shows. However, a major show needs the early advice of an expert who often can offer good ideas for the staging. In a store the display director frequently takes over this role, since he is experienced in lighting effects.

The Commentator

More and more fashion shows are being staged without commentary, but there are times when a commentator is desirable. This subject is discussed in detail in Chapter 11.

Stage Manager

When a fashion show is given staging effects — sets, props, and action — the responsibility for managing the stage needs to be fixed with one person. He sees that everything is in order, that the curtain is opened and closed at the right moment, that sets are changed quickly, that the right members of the cast are backstage, and that all cues are followed. Also he handles any slips or emergencies.

In a major city, professionals are available. Otherwise, anyone who is thoroughly familiar with the show may assume this responsibility. It might be the display manager of a store if he doesn't have another assignment or the assistant to the fashion director. Desirable qualities for a stage manager are the ability to think and act quickly, to keep calm, and to handle the cast and crew with firmness and diplomacy. In some cities and buildings it may be necessary for the stage manager to be a union member.

Backstage Crew

The stage manager specifies and preferably selects the crew he will need to handle everything that goes on backstage. This includes operating the curtain, changing sets, and handling props. Enough crew members are needed to make split-second changes, but not so many that they get in the way and add to the confusion. Each person's duties must be clearly defined.

Dressing-Room Staff

Let no one believe that the dressing room is just a place where models go to change their clothes. It is a whole organization within itself, completely discussed in Chapter 8. It must be staffed with quick workers who know how a model should look when she goes on a runway, and who are able to handle emergencies without hysteria. This is probably the least glamorous job of the whole show because these workers rarely see any of the show unless they sneak out for a peek at the finale after the last model leaves the dressing room.

Fitter-Alteration Hand

Clothes must fit the models as perfectly as possible. Lengths must be correct. It is better to eliminate an outfit than to let it go on the runway looking wrong. Thus a fitter should be present to take care of any necessary alterations.

A BUDGET IS ESSENTIAL

Many inexperienced persons believe that a fashion show costs little or nothing. On the contrary, even informal modeling involves costs and sometimes substantial ones. One fashion director has estimated that the simplest little show costs at least $500. As the show becomes more elaborate, the costs go up. Probably the most expensive show on record is the Milliken Breakfast Show where a budget of a million dollars is allotted (including the food served).

Most shows are given a budget amount that is then allocated to the different expenses involved. The size of the budget naturally determines how big the show may be. Few are so lucky as to be able to plan a show and then request the amount of money needed.

Retail stores plan their budgets on a six-month basis—February through July and August through January. Any fashion shows within those periods are scheduled, or at least provided for, at the time the budgets are compiled.

There are certain major expenses that take large sums of money, and there are numerous incidentals that can add up to a sizable amount. Also there are always emergencies and unexpected expenses that pop up. An amount for such contingencies should be included.

The following comprehensive list covers the expenses of a fashion show. Naturally, it is unlikely that every one of these would be incurred in one show, but it may serve as a checklist. The chairman or producer must be able to foresee which expenses will occur and estimate as accurately as possible the needed amounts. Costs of a past show are helpful to refer to in estimating an upcoming one. Also it is possible to obtain accurate estimates from some of the free-lance persons involved and from some of the suppliers.

The Fashion-Show Budget

Room rental
  For show
  For rehearsals (or rehearsal hall)
Invitations
  Printing
  Mailing costs
Advertising or other publicity
  Press releases and pictures
Tickets
Programs
Specialists' fees (see staff requirements in this chapter)
Musicians
Talent
Electrical and lighting equipment
Stage sets
Props
Runway (including setting up)
  Construction or rental of runway
  Carpenters to set up
  Fabric to cover
  Upholsterer to cover
Models' fees
Costs in connection with merchandise
  Alterations
  Cleaning and pressing before show
  Pressing at show (including irons, ironing boards)
Photographer
Favors
Table centerpieces or decorations
Guards
Porters
Trucking
  Clothes
  Sets and props
  Other equipment
Amplification (PA system and microphones)
Projection (if any)
Dressing room supplies
Rentals
  Racks for clothes
  Tables for accessories
  Mirrors
Telephone calls

Checkroom tips (or guests may pay)
Restroom tips (or guests may pay)
All other gratuities
Food and beverages
  For guests
  For models and staff
Any taxes due

DELEGATE RESPONSIBILITIES

Schedule the first meeting to plan a fashion show well in advance of the show date — how far ahead is governed by the size of the show. For a major production, six months ahead is not too early. Last-minute planning should be avoided because it may lead to heavy additional expenses and it certainly will not lead to a good show.

The person who is in charge of the entire show should prepare, for this first meeting, a typed outline of (1) everything that must be done in producing the show, (2) who will be responsible for each activity, and (3) a time schedule with deadlines for each step. The theme of the show should be discussed at this meeting so that invitations or advertising may be planned. Any bookings that must be made early (such as bookings for music or models) should be agreed on at this time if possible.

The entire staff that will work on the show does not have to be present at this meeting, but copies of the schedule should be sent to each member so that work may proceed.

HOW LONG A SHOW

The desired length of the show must be established early in the planning process because it governs so many other aspects (for instance, how much staging, how many models, and the like). A straight showing of fashions without any staging or entertainment should not last more than 30 minutes (40, at the most). About 60 to 75 outfits can be modeled easily in half an hour. You can show 80 to 100 in 40 minutes, but a shorter show is preferred.

If the show has entertainment, 40 minutes to an hour is a good length. This time must be divided between the modeling and the entertainment to arrive at the number of outfits to select. Certainly the clothes deserve most of the time (unless the show is pure entertainment), and the entertainment and staging should be used to enhance the fashions. A good way to estimate how many outfits can be shown in the allotted

FASHION SHOW EXPENDITURES

(Prepare in duplicate. Send one copy to Merchandise Manager's office)

Name of show _____   Date of show _____

Location _____

Audience _____
                  open to public or special group

		planned attendance	actual attendance

		BUDGET	ACTUAL
I.	FASHION OFFICE		
	1. Assemble and return — labor @ $2 per hour	_____	_____
	2. Model fees ____ x $ ____	_____	_____
	3. Labor — dressers	_____	_____
	4. Fashion guest	_____	_____
	5. Transportation	_____	_____
II.	MERCHANDISE EXPENSE		
	1. Alterations and dressing	_____	_____
	2. Damages (markdowns)	_____	_____
	3. Lost or stolen	_____	_____
III.	ADVERTISING		
	1. Store advertising	_____	_____
	2. Programs	_____	_____
	3. Tickets (admission, door prize)	_____	_____
	4. Publicity photographs	_____	_____
	5. Radio or T.V.	_____	_____
	6. Display cards, signs, table tents	_____	_____
IV.	DECORATION		
	1. Display — labor	_____	_____
	2. Display — props, flowers, etc.	_____	_____
V.	LIGHTING		
	1. Spotlights	_____	_____
	2. Electricians (labor)	_____	_____

Budget form used by one retail department store, as budgeted and as actually spent.

Organization : _____   Date : _____   Time : _____   Place : _____   Expected : _____

Restaurant	Refreshments	Served by	Candles		Special instructions
Protection	Elevators	Entrance / exits			Special instructions
Display	Stage and background	Lights	Music	Mike	Dressing area	Special instructions
Mrs. Leonard	Chairs	Porters			Special instructions

One retail department store uses this mimeographed chart to record responsibilities in connection with a fashion show.

time is to figure two to two-and-a-half outfits per minute, governed by the extent of the commentary and the length of the runway.

Sometimes you may have to work in reverse. The clothes to be shown may be specified first and the show time estimated from that. For example, there may be a designer collection of 30 outfits that can be modeled in 15 minutes, but you want to give the collection more importance by having a 30-minute show. The problem is to pad the show without dragging it out and making it boring.

A survey among fashion directors of the outstanding stores in the United States revealed their preferences as to number of outfits that make a good show:

Type of Show	Number of Outfits
Small informal show in the department	18 to 24
Regular fashion show in or out of store	30 to 60
Big special show	70 to 80
Big spectacular	80 to 100

BOOK MODELS EARLY

In areas where models are at a premium, book them as early as possible in order to obtain the best ones who are usually in heavy demand. Chapter 10 provides complete information about models. Remember, when planning, that you will need the models three times:

1. For fittings.
2. For rehearsals.
3. For the show.

FITTING AND ACCESSORIZING

Fittings must be carefully timed—early enough to allow sufficient time for alterations and late enough to be able to include the newest clothes. If clothes are taken out of stock in a store, they cannot be kept out too long because of the loss of sales and the possibility of the stock becoming stale. About a week before show time should accommodate all of these needs.

For a big show of 100 outfits, the work will go faster and more smoothly if you line up the following staff to be on hand:

A fashion director (to be the final authority).

Two assistants to select clothes for models and dress them.
One assistant to pick shoes and hosiery.
One assistant to pick other accessories.
One or two fitter/alteration hands.
One assistant to write fitting sheets.
One assistant to bag accessories.

This maximum staff may be scaled down to fit the situation and the number of models. For some very small shows or for informal modeling, experienced models may even fit and accessorize themselves. A good professional model has a feeling for what she can show best and how it should be put together. Of course, nonprofessionals should never be left to fit themselves.

Equipment for the Fitting Room

Assemble all supplies beforehand so that fittings (which are expensive) may move along as quickly as possible. A little platform about one foot off the floor is helpful for marking hems. This also enables the fashion director to judge how the lengths will look on a runway. Remember: the clothes will be seen at a height of about three feet off the floor with the audience seated and looking up at the models. Sometimes a runway as high as six feet is used when the audience is standing. Elevating the model during fitting also makes it easier to decide what kind of hosiery and undergear are needed if the garment is very short.

An assortment of additional supplies should be on hand for fittings:

Fitting sheets in triplicate—a set for each outfit	Extra hangers
	Shoe horns
Carbon paper	Cellophane tape
Ball-point pens	Stapling machines
Shopping bags for accessories (one per outfit)	Felt markers
	Cleansing tissues
Hem marker or yardstick	Tissue paper
Tape measures	Band-Aids
Pins and pincushions	Aspirin
Tailor's chalk	Plenty of coffee for crew and models!
Scissors	
Masking tape for shoes	

The Use of Fitting Sheets

For a well-organized show, fill out a fitting sheet in triplicate for each garment as it is fitted on a model and accessorized. In addition to providing a record of the outfit, it comes in handy for many other purposes:

FALL TRENDS SHOW — JUNE 6TH, 1969

GRAND BALLROOM, WALDORF-ASTORIA

FALL TRENDS SHOW — JUNE 6TH, 1969

GRAND BALLROOM, WALDORF-ASTORIA

FALL TRENDS SHOW — JUNE 6TH, 1969

GRAND BALLROOM, WALDORF-ASTORIA

FALL TRENDS SHOW — JUNE 6TH, 1969

GRAND BALLROOM, WALDORF-ASTORIA

SCENE*_____

MODEL_____ ORDER OF APPEARANCE_____

MANUFACTURER_____

OUTFIT_____

_____

_____

ALTERATIONS_____

_____

_____

ACCESSORIES (MANUFACTURER AND DESCRIPTION)

JEWELRY:

SHOES:	STOCKINGS:
HAT OR HAIR RIBBON:	SCARF:
BAG:	GLOVES:
BELT:	FOUNDATIONS:
OTHER:	

SPECIAL NOTES/PROPS:

Fitting sheet to be filled out for one outfit fitted on one model. In triplicate, white original is pinned to garment; pink copy is pinned to accessory bag; yellow copy goes to fashion show director. A fourth blue copy may be added for show director or for general use by show staff.

Notations about how clothes/accessories are to be worn.
Notations of alterations to be made.
List of accessories chosen.
Notation of accessories still to be obtained.
Checklist for accessory bag.
Reference for fashion director and assistants.

One copy of the sheet, after it has been completed, should be pinned to the garment. Clothes to be altered should be assembled as fitted on one rack, while those requiring no alterations are hung on other racks in numerical order.

A second copy of the fitting sheet should be pinned securely to the shopping bag containing the accessories for that outfit. The third copy can go onto a clipboard or in a looseleaf notebook for the fashion director and her assistants to use in completing accessories and keeping track of where the merchandise is. A sample fitting sheet is illustrated.

For a smaller show, a much simpler form may be used successfully. There may be one sheet for each model, covering all garments she is to wear in order of appearance. Or there may be only one large sheet or sheets on which all models are listed in order of appearance with their garments. Examples of these forms are also illustrated. When these shortcuts are used, each garment must be tagged with the lineup number and the model's name.

Arranging the Merchandise for Fittings

Arrange the clothes in the numerical order of the lineup on racks that are easily accessible. Lay out all accessories on tables by classification and type—shoes together by type and color, belts together, jewelry together, and so on.

Basic Wardrobe of Accessories for a Store

Any retail store (or any company or organization that regularly produces fashion shows) should keep a basic wardrobe of seasonal accessories on hand. This will expedite fittings and will save stock merchandise from damage or loss, thereby saving money. These accessories can be used over and over during a season. Five types are the backbone of an accessory wardrobe:

1. *Gloves.* In prevailing fashion lengths . . . in neutral white, beige, black, navy, brown, and a few fashion colors . . . sizes 6½ to 7½, or stretch that fit all . . . launder washable gloves after each show.
2. *Jewelry.* Pieces in the prevailing fashion types, such as earrings and bracelets . . . in the current fashion media and stones . . . in types for

NAME_____ DATE_____

Shoes _____
Hat _____
Bag _____
Gloves _____
Jewelry_____
Misc. _____

Shoes _____
Hat _____
Bag _____
Gloves _____
Jewelry_____
Misc. _____

Shoes_____
Hat _____
Bag _____
Gloves _____
Jewelry_____
Misc. _____

Shoes _____
Hat _____
Bag _____
Gloves _____
Jewelry_____
Misc. _____

Shoes _____
Hat _____
Bag _____
Gloves _____
Jewelry_____
Misc. _____

A well-organized fitting sheet on which as many as five of one model's outfits may be listed.

different occasions . . . all with runway appeal (important enough to show up).

3. *Shoes*. Types for sportswear, daytime and street wear, cocktail and evening . . . boots . . . basic and fashion colors and media . . . bridal show shoes in white and dyed . . . sizes 6½-A to 8½-A.

4. *Hosiery*. Since this is one type of merchandise that cannot be sold after worn by a model, it is essential to have a wardrobe of stockings, socks, pantyhose, leotards, body stockings . . . basic and fashion colors and patterns . . . stretch to fit all when possible, or sizes 8½ to 10½ or even 11, regular and long . . . launder after each show.

5. *Scarfs*. A variety of sizes and shapes (square, long, and others in fashion) . . . in solids and patterns . . . can use slightly faded ones from windows.

Handbags and hats are costly, so these are better borrowed from stock as needed. Shoes are also actually better taken from stock, except that many shoe departments fear that shoes will be damaged or soiled so that they cannot be sold as new when returned to stock. However, a shoe department should realize that all fashion departments take markdowns for promotion purposes.

There are other items that are handy to have in the fitting room:

hair ribbons and ornaments
sunglasses
flowers
hairpieces
umbrellas
girdles, bras, slips, formal slips
swimsuit briefs

The fashion coordinator of a store needs a budget for transferring and charging these accessories to her department. Through the hosiery buyer, she can sometimes save a bit of money by wangling stockings from a manufacturer in return for runway and/or program credit.

Matching the Fashions to the Models

The fitting staff may know the models so well that they can instantly pull out the fashions that each can wear best. However, there are always size and change problems. A garment may not be available in the size to fit the model it would look best on. A model's changes may be too close together. For these reasons, it may be necessary to make very slight

ACCESSORY LIST

MODEL'S NAME _____   SHOW _____

NO.	COSTUME DESCRIPTION	GLOVES	NO. JEWELRY	STOCKINGS	MISCELLANEOUS

Two forms used together by one store; an accessory list for all outfits to be modeled by one model, and a fit sheet that may include the outfits for one model, or for more than one.

changes in the lineup during the fitting, but major shifts are to be avoided as they will breed bigger problems.

The numbers between a model's changes depend on how professional she is, how far away the dressing room is, and how good the

FIT SHEETS

SHOW_____   DATE OF SHOW _____

MODEL	STYLE	DEPT.	SIZE	DESCRIPTION	PRICE

dressing room staff is. There are several guidelines that may help in estimating:

- It is preferable not to have a model change within one sequence. If it is necessary, be sure it is a long sequence so that she will have adequate time, and she will not cause amusement by almost following herself out.

SHOW:			DATE:	
NAME	OUTFIT	HAT	SHOES	OTHER
No.				
No.				
No.				
No.				
No.				
No.				

A simple ruled form that may be filled in as a fitting sheet, or as a sheet for listing the clothes in lineup order.

- Models in a bridal show require more time for changes, so more numbers between appearances must be allowed.
- If a large group of models is scheduled to come out together, such as eight models choreographed for a special routine, more models overall may be needed to allow for this group's changing at one

time. There must be enough models following them to allow for changing. The alternative is to have a special feature of some kind between sequences to provide the extra dressing time.

• A general rule for a show of 40 or more pieces is to allow ten numbers between a change. However, a long runway or a distant dressing room may require a wider span. Each model can handle four or more changes. A show of 40 could be handled easily by ten girls, or even as few as six. Nonprofessionals need more time so this must be taken into consideration.

As a guide, a group of outstanding store fashion directors specifies the following approximate number of models needed for shows of certain sizes.

Number of Pieces in Show	Number of Models Needed
30	6
40	6 to 10
50	8 to 10
60	10 to 12
70	12 to 14, or up to 20

When a model looks well in an outfit selected for her, enter her name on the lineup. The fitter should mark and pin any alterations. The accessory assistants can make their selections and try them on the model. These should then be noted on the fitting sheet.

Assembling the Accessories for each Model

Many fashion directors have their own favorite ways of keeping together the accessories for each model and each outfit she wears. The trusty shopping bag (a large size about 16 in. high, by 12 in. wide, with gusset about 7 in.) is inexpensive and probably more effective and easier to handle than any other method. They may be hooked over the hangers with the clothes and thus go right on the racks.

As each outfit is fitted and accessorized on a model, put the accessories carefully into a shopping bag so that they will not be crushed. Any accessories that have to be obtained should be noted on the fitting sheet, along with the alteration instructions.

The model's name is then prominently written on the shopping bag (a felt marker is perfect for this), together with the number of the outfit in the lineup:

16
Mari Davis

If no alterations are necessary, the bag can be hooked over the hanger and the outfit placed on a completed rack. When garments go to alteration, put the accessory bags together in a safe place. They can be hooked over empty hangers and put on racks or stored elsewhere.

Some fashion directors use other methods. One way is to put small accessories, such as jewelry and gloves, in a small paper bag, hats in a hatbox or pinned to the outfit (awkward on the racks), and shoes in boxes. This is too scattered for efficiency. Another method is to put everything for one outfit or one model in a hatbox with a list of what goes with what. This is not ideal because the boxes take space and must be handled separately. Still another way is to distribute accessories to models' dressing tables with lists. This takes extra time in the dressing room and is guaranteed to generate problems. Least desirable method, to be avoided, is to lay all accessories on tables and "throw" them on the models as they dress. The show, too, will surely look thrown together.

A Word about Alterations

Every care must be taken in the fittings to keep alterations to an absolute minimum. Aside from the fact that alterations may cause clothes to have to be marked down after the show, this service is very expensive and someone must pay for it. The fact that a store has fitters and alteration hands doesn't mean that the service is free. The costs will be charged against the show budget and credited to the alteration department, even though no money actually changes hands.

A manufacturer may be able to have the fashions in a new line he plans to show made for the models who will wear them. This is, of course, a distinct advantage.

If these channels are not available, a good dressmaker may be employed to handle the fittings. Be sure she is professional and fast. Some basis for pricing should be arrived at before the fittings start.

PLANNING THE SETTINGS

Whatever is done in the way of staging must be able to be accomplished within the framework of the facilities available, and the time allotted for setting up and taking down. Planning must start as early as possible to allow for construction without incurring overtime payments.

The setting must look professional. Better to show against curtains or no-seam display paper than to look like "loving hands at home" which will make the clothes look dowdy.

Since stage settings can run into sizable sums of money, a fairly accurate estimate in writing should be obtained before commissioning the work.

A point that is often overlooked is your responsibility for "striking" (taking down) a set and removing it within a certain time after the show. This is usually the case in a rented ballroom or hall where other events may follow close on the heels of the fashion show. Provision must be made for workers to do this, and possibly also for trucking and storing. You can't just walk away and leave it—or you may receive a substantial bill for disposal.

PLANNING AND BOOKING THE MUSIC

Popular local music groups are usually booked for months ahead. Therefore, this is one of the first steps to be taken at the outset of planning a show. The music possibilities are discussed in Chapter 7. Reference is made to it here to emphasize that this is an important part of the planning of a fashion show.

PLANNING THE LIGHTING

Lighting and electrical problems are covered in Chapters 5 and 7. Since lighting is a part of the staging, it should be discussed during the initial planning so that advantage may be taken of its many dramatic possibilities.

UNION RULES MUST BE OBSERVED

Unions that may be encountered in producing fashion shows have been mentioned in Chapter 5. This is a subject to check at the very outset because it can control many things.

It isn't only that you may be required to use union help throughout. Certain unions may be specified. An organization giving a big fashion show in the Waldorf-Astoria in New York thought it was following the rules by employing a union trucker to deliver the clothes to the hotel ballroom. They found themselves with a sticky problem when they were met at the hotel door by representatives of the theatrical trucking union who claimed they were the only ones who could bring clothes to a show, even though it was not a true theatrical production.

A similar incident happened to another organization that attempted to have a trucker deliver their stage set to a hotel ballroom. A union representative who met this truck simply said, "You're not having any

Two dancers in the Milliken Breakfast Show take instructions from Michael Bennett, right, the noted Broadway choreographer, during the grueling rehearsals of several weeks' duration.

Choreographer Michael Bennett believes in thorough rehearsals for several weeks preceding the Milliken Breakfast Show. Here, he leads a dance number in a rehearsal hall.

show tonight." The show staff spent a harrowing day negotiating before they were permitted to go ahead with the show.

Both organizations were innocent in that they were not deliberately trying to circumvent unions. They simply had not inquired into the subject, and were not even aware that they should.

REHEARSALS ARE THE FINAL STEP TO A GOOD SHOW

The last step before the show is rehearsals, but these must be planned and scheduled from the beginning because of the necessity of booking rehearsal time, models, and staff early.

Even professionals need rehearsals, to say nothing of amateurs. Naturally, amateurs need more. Special numbers of any kind can and should be separately rehearsed even before rehearsal of the whole company. If the models are amateurs, they should be rehearsed in modeling on the runway.

Try to hold a final dress rehearsal in the actual room of the show just before the show. This should be finished about an hour before the show begins, so that everyone can rest a bit and get reorganized for the big event.

7

How to Put Showmanship into the Fashion Show

Since the fashion show is a "show" involving "performers" on a stage, platform, or runway before an audience, the producer takes on the basic responsibilities of the producer of a Broadway show. In other words, he or she employs all of the tools of showmanship. This immediately indicates two basic ingredients:

1. *Professionalism.* While models, musicians, entertainers, and everyone else involved in a show may be amateurs, the production must be handled in a professional way. It must have a plan, be adequately rehearsed, and be presented with assurance. The number of pieces shown and the length of the entire show must be right, and there must be a balance between fashions and entertainment.

2. *Excitement.* A Broadway show without excitement closes very quickly after it opens, or it may close on the road and never see Broadway. While a fashion show is usually a one-time event, it has to hold the interest and attendance of the audience until the very end. In fact, the audience should be left with an appetite for more, rather than with indigestion. Every step of the fashion show must make its contribution to the excitement—from the booking of the place to the final curtain.

GIVE THE SHOW A CATCHY TITLE

Like a good title for a play or a book, a good title for a fashion show can "sell" the show. It can also set the theme for the whole show, or the theme of the show may suggest the title.

A good name for the show makes the publicity easier. It can be used in the invitations to whet interest and attendance, in newspaper ads to stimulate attendance, and in publicity releases to generate pickup by the press.

The almost full-page advertisement of Best & Co. to announce the initiation of evening cycling in New York's Central Park and their "Cycles in Fashion" show to celebrate the event.

Here are actual examples of good titles that have been used to theme fashion shows:

- "Cycles in Fashion," a show on bicycles given by Best's of New York to celebrate the evening openings of Central Park to cyclists.
- "The Big Wheels of Fall," an Abraham & Straus teen-age fashion show of pants modeled on bicycles in Prospect Park in Brooklyn.
- "English Accent," Alexander's showing of English male fashions in the New York showroom of Jaguar cars.
- "Pup-Fashions," a showing of designer clothes with coordinated dog fashions, given at lunch in a New York restaurant.
- "The Beautiful Waste Makers," an all-paper fashion show in Chicago sponsored by The Fashion Group.
- "Fashion Fur-Cast," a fur show, also by The Fashion Group of Chicago.
- "Why Men Stay at Home," an at-home collection of clothes shown by The Fashion Group of Philadelphia.
- "The Best of America," a showing of high fashions and fine horses at famous Fairview Stables, given by Myers Brothers of Springfield, Illinois.
- "The Tinseltown Hollywood Thirties," a showing of bridal fashions at Dayton's of Minneapolis.
- "Metropolitan Moods," a sophisticated benefit show by Robinson's of Los Angeles.
- "A Day on the Delta," by Rich's of Atlanta, complete with Mississippi riverboat music.
- "What to Wear to the Earthquake," a show by Saks Fifth Avenue of San Francisco that humorously took advantage of earthquake predictions in April 1969.

It's easy to see how almost all of these titles were suggested by the fashions to be shown. The titles could easily apply to the theme for the entire show, invitations, program, and publicity.

A THEMATIC IDEA IS HALF THE WORK

One thematic idea carried through the entire show makes a more cohesive production, as long as you don't beat the idea to death. It is used only as a tool to a better show, and must never be allowed to confine you too narrowly. The opening and closing scenes might be pegged to the theme, with the middle part of the show carried by the fashions

seventeen

SEE HOW SHE RACES TO THE SEVENTEEN FALL TRENDS SHOW
WHERE SHE'LL LEARN THE NEWEST, MOST EXCITING FASHION
SECRETS OF THE 1966 BACK-TO-SCHOOL SEASON.
SEE HOW SHE USES THIS INFORMATION TO SAVE THE FASHION
LIVES OF MILLIONS OF TEEN-AGE GIRLS.
JOIN THE SIDE OF RIGHT! COME TO THE GRAND BALLROOM
OF THE WALDORF ASTORIA ON JUNE 3RD AT 4:30 P.M.
AND SEE SUPERTEEN IN ACTION
(SHE'S FLYING, BUT YOU CAN WALK RIGHT THROUGH THE
50TH STREET—PARK AVENUE ENTRANCE)

**SEND
COUPON
TODAY!**

I WANT TO BE WITH SUPERTEEN ON THE SIDE OF RIGHT
(ESPECIALLY IF IT'S FASHION RIGHT).
PLEASE SEND ME A TICKET TO THE SEVENTEEN FALL
TRENDS SHOW.

NAME_____
TITLE_____
COMPANY_____
ADDRESS_____
CITY_____STATE_____ZIP____

This illustration demonstrates how a timely theme can be carried out through all printed material in connection with a fashion show. *Seventeen* Magazine takes inspiration from the Broadway production of "Superman" for its "Superteen" fashion show: (a) (*above*) an invitation with reservation card attached; (b) (*right*) ticket; (c) (*p. 114*) program. As show opener, "Superteen" flies across the stage.

themselves. The thematic idea is a platform for mounting the fashion story.

The bridal show mentioned in the preceding section is an excellent example of using a theme to set off the merchandise. Bridal fashions are very much the same, and it's difficult to plan a different kind of bridal show. When Dayton's show was given in 1967, there was tremendous popular interest in movies per se and particularly in old movies of the

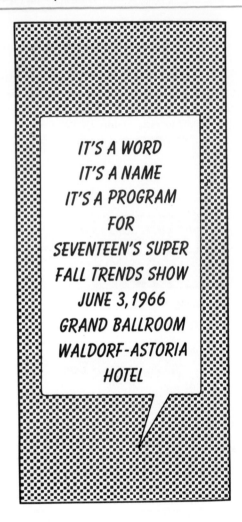

1930s. Also, that decade produced some of the most glamorous movie stars of all time. Bridal fashions are glamorous; brides are stars. Result: "The Tinseltown Hollywood Thirties," a perfect tie-in idea for advertising, invitations, stage setting, music, programs, with old movie clips as background entertainment.

It's easy to find ideas for themes. The problem is in choosing the best one for the specific purpose from the myriad available. Themes may come from almost everywhere:

- *Current Events.* Watch newspapers and news magazines for current events that provide the most obvious themes possible. This can be an event of wide interest such as an election, an exposition, an exhibition, a big sports event. It may be the opening of a new movie such as the 1968 release of "Star" that triggered many fashion show themes. Several gala benefits were based on "Star" with the original Donald Brooks costumes modeled, along with his current fashions.

  A new play might be just the thing, like "How to Succeed in Business Without Really Trying" which opened in the early 1960s and later became a movie. There couldn't have been a better handle for a business girls' show. "Your Own Thing," a New York off-Broadway musical became the basic idea for many young shows in 1968, the year of its greatest popularity.

- *Seasons.* Although not the most original idea, the season can become the theme, such as "Salute to Spring," "Winter Wonderland," or "Holiday Happenings." There are times when merchandise from a group of designers or a group of stores must be used together in a show. Often this means a conglomeration of many ideas that are not necessarily compatible with each other. This is the time when a general "umbrella" title such as these may be useful. The San Francisco "Fashion Port of Fall" show is such an example.

- *Holidays.* Some holidays offer better ideas than others. Washington's Birthday and Fourth of July are filled with patriotic lore that can be translated into a cracking show. New Year's is good for a "New Year, New You" beauty-oriented show (new fashions are at a low point at this time of year). Unusual events in history that are not real holidays can be amusing, such as the Oklahoma Run on April 22nd (1889), which could theme a western show.

- *Music.* New popular releases, show tunes, or even light or grand operas sometimes provide good fashion show themes. The Beatles' "Sergeant Pepper" album set off young uniform-inspired fashions in shows in 1968. Soul music has themed "Soul Fashions" shows. A title such as "The Fashion Beat" could be used for a show in which a different type of music or a different tune could theme each sequence.

- *Art.* Special exhibitions have long been a fashion show idea factory. The Museum of Modern Art's 1968–1969 "The Machine as Seen at the End of the Mechanical Age" was an appropriate idea for any contemporary show. Their "Word and Image" poster exhibition in 1968 was another idea translatable into a show theme, such as

"Fashion Posters." Often material is available from a local museum to add interest to the show, and the museum is pleased with the additional publicity.

- *Place.* Sometimes the locale of a show can become the theme. The annual show to generate interest in the United Hospital Fund in New York was given several times at the Rockefeller Center Skating Rink. With models on skates, theme of the show was "Fashions on Ice." Lamson's of Toledo produced one of the most original teen-age fashion shows on a new strip of Highway 475 not yet opened to traffic. They appropriately named the show, "Alive on 475."

- *Travel.* With the world on the move, travel is a sure-fire theme if used at the right time and for the right clothes. "The Island Hoppers" or "Season in the Sun" could theme a resort show in the winter. "Sail A-Weigh" might signal a summer show of fashions for shore areas. "The High Fliers" might be a packable show for jet travelers.

- *Colors.* While a good show generally needs a variety of colors, an unusual show could be produced by using a color theme whenever a color or colors have special fashion importance. All black and white can make the most dramatic show imaginable—all fashions in black and white against black and white settings. Sharp color accents for relief and punctuation can be introduced in accessories and props. White raincoats might be accessorized with black umbrellas and bright red or yellow scarfs. Call the show "Fashion Chiaroscuro." A "Fashion in the Pink" show could feature fashions from pale pink to rich red. "Get the Fashion Blues" could confine fashions to all the blue tones.

- *Audience Interests.* Perhaps there is a common denominator among the interests of the prospective audience that can be used effectively as a theme. Most men and boys like sports and cars—and girls!—so any of these subjects can be a show theme. "The Growing Fashions" would be appropriate for a ladies' garden club audience.

Any one of the ideas suggested, or that you may think of, can provide showmanship in most of the elements of the show, making the whole project easier and more exciting:

> publicity, ads, invitations
> program
> setting
> props
> music
> giveaways and favors

For an audience of young movie buffs, Jordan Marsh of Miami turns a fashion show into a sneak preview in a "Theatre" by use of blowups of stars, stanchions, and chains.

THE CLOTHES MUST BE DRAMATIC

Unless clothes for a fashion show are chosen with stage presence in mind, the show will end up being much ado about nothing. Although the clothes must relate to the audience (which may not consist of fashion plates), they cannot be a dull parade. They must have some excitement and news value, and must stand out on a stage against settings and under strong lights.

In selecting clothes, forget about ordinary fashions that have reached volume status because they are not news and will bore the audience. Be sure each piece meets these requirements:

- It is new.
- It has a fashion reason for being in the show.
- It will look important on a stage.

Any good fashion show can stand a few "showpieces" that make the audience gasp when they come out. These may be clothes that the audi-

The silver look in fashion is made even more exciting when five models wear the same fashion and wheel silver motorcycles on stage in a *Seventeen* Magazine show.

ence would never under any circumstances buy or wear, but that will entertain them and make them talk. Something that is a little extreme in styling, or that is a dramatically new departure, or that has an extremely high price can impart this kind of drama to the show.

Accentuate the Positive

It is always best to show what is correct, rather than to try to show the wrong look versus the right look. Otherwise, there is the chance that some of those in the audience may like the wrong look and carry that impression away with them.

The classic example of this danger is the story of a fashion show in London some years ago that was attended by the wife of the Prime Minister. When right and wrong models came out together to demonstrate the understated look that was preferred to the overdone look, the commentator explained why one was right and the other wrong. Mrs. Prime Minister, seated in the front row, leaned forward and whispered how very pretty she thought Miss Wrong looked.

Accessorize for Drama

Choosing accessories for a fashion show is just as important as selecting the clothes themselves. Sometimes, when merchandise that lacks excitement must be shown for some reason, the accessories become even more important than the clothes because they can add the drama that the clothes lack. This does not mean flashy or extreme accessorizing. It means using new and interesting pieces that are appropriate for the clothes and in good taste.

Yves St. Laurent, one of the greatest of the Paris designers, believes so strongly in the importance of the total look that when designing a new collection, he tries one accessory after another on his models until he achieves just the right effect. He says that accessories can make or break the balance of a dress. St. Laurent also considers makeup, hair styling, and even perfume or eau de toilette an integral part of the accessorizing.

The worst possible mistake in producing a fashion show is to ask the models, whether professional or not, to bring their own accessories. Even shoes should be provided for them. Although their feet may not be seen by the entire audience, the wrong shoes can ruin the appearance of the entire outfit faster than anything else.

Drama can sometimes be added by using the same accessories for a group of models. It might be a group showing different raincoats, but all twirling the same kind of umbrella and wearing the same style in

An all gold-and-white fashion show is dramatic, produced by Courtaulds of London. The elegantly simple setting is in keeping with the beautiful gowns shown. Courtesy of Michael Whittaker of London.

One accessory worn by all models, a western cowboy hat, points up the western theme threading through the fashions in a scene from the Milliken Breakfast Show.

boots. The same knit cap and long, flying scarf might give an exciting look to a scene of campus coats. Long feather boas might lend excitement to a clutch of 1930s party dresses.

Since the fashions are the show, tip-to-toe coordination is essential — and that bit of fragrance that St. Laurent likes can be the finishing touch that makes each total look really complete, and helps each model to feel special.

STRUCTURING THE SCENES FOR DRAMA

Excitement and interest are generated by the new and different, not by the ordinary and mundane. Thus a fashion show needs news. Before selecting any clothes, list the new fashion ideas along with the accepted current fashion themes. This list is the fashion story you will tell to the audience and becomes the sequences (scenes or acts) of the show.

While you can use as many fashion ideas as there are, it is best to edit the list down to a minimum of five or six, or a maximum of eight to ten. There must be enough to make a varied show, but not so much that the audience is confused by too many courses at the feast.

Blend Low Key and High Key

The next step is to arrange the sequences in an order that provides an interesting pace for the show and maintains audience interest. This means blending the low key ideas with the high key ideas, so that you offer variety and at the same time work up to a climax.

Unlike the theater which frequently opens in a quiet way to give the audience a few moments to get settled in their seats, a fashion show should "grab" the audience with the first model. Select a new fashion idea for this opening sequence and present it with drama. Alternate the subsequent sequences between groups of fashions that are already accepted and the brand-new ones. End on a high note of news, beauty, or drama that sends the audience away with a positive memory of a good show and a feeling of good will.

One big and expensive fashion show given before an audience of 1800 in a New York hotel ballroom was a failure because it opened with the biggest fashion news of the time and worked steadily down to a final sequence of the dullest, most uninteresting clothes in the show. The lights went up on an audience of yawners who departed with grumbles.

The thematic fashion sequences for a Spring 1970 young show might be paced this way:

Scene 1 (opening)	The Slithery Slink (the big fashion news of slinky, clinging fabrics in dresses and sportswear)
Scene 2	The String Thing (string color in exciting clothes, but not big news)
Scene 3	Color-splashed Jeans (tie-dyed jeans with T-shirts—the least exciting merchandise, but necessary to include because of the wide acceptance of jeans and T-shirts)
Scene 4	The No-Coat Coat (the significant new fashion of the soft unconstructed coat)
Scene 5	The Wide-Open Spaces (the continuing fashion of the midriff, interpreted in new ways)
Scene 6 (climax)	The Play of Purple (date and party clothes in color variations from lilac and mauve to deep purple, ending the show on a note of beauty and romance)

Slotting in the Clothes

Try to divide the number of clothes to be shown fairly evenly among the sequences, but don't have each exactly the same. If you have 75 outfits to be broken into six sequences, an interesting allocation might be:

Scene 1	The Slithery Slink	14 Outfits
Scene 2	The String Thing	11 Outfits
Scene 3	Color-Splashed Jeans	9 Outfits
Scene 4	The No-Coat Coat	12 Outfits

| Scene 5 | The Wide-Open Spaces | 11 Outfits |
| Scene 6 | The Play of Purple | 18 Outfits |

This breakdown provides enough clothes and models in the first and last scenes to make an impact. Scenes 2 and 3 are shorter to prevent boredom. Then Scene 4 (which should be one of your important fashion ideas) is a semiclimax at midpoint. Scene 5 quiets down with fewer models, while Scene 6 builds to a splashing climax and finale, possibly with the addition of some boys as escorts for the girls in their party clothes.

THE LINEUP TELLS A STORY

When all of the clothes have been chosen and slotted into sequences, the next step is to make the "lineup." This is the exact order in which they will appear on the runway. The lineup must provide the most exciting and dramatic presentation possible:

- Open a scene with new and exciting merchandise.
- Tuck the least exciting pieces into the middle of the group. However, if it is a long sequence, keep varying the merchandise from exciting to quiet or the show will die.
- Always end a segment on a high note with something newsy or dramatic.

The Mechanics of the Lineup

As the clothes are slotted into the appropriate sequences, type a 5 in. by 8 in. title card for each sequence:

SCENE 1.   THE SLITHERY SLINK
(14 Outfits)

Type a card for each outfit that is selected and file it behind the appropriate divider card, with the following information:

SCENE 1.   THE SLITHERY SLINK

Beige/white Art Déco print on acetate
jersey wrapped and tied tunic   **$19.95**

with

Matching flared pants, elasticized waist	$19.95

and

White acetate jersey 9-ft fringed scarf	$10.00

This deck of cards may be kept by the fashion director in a box or just with a rubber band. As work on the show progresses and models are fitted into the clothes, additional notes may be made on the cards. Also, there will undoubtedly be changes in the merchandise for various reasons before the show is finalized. Frequently, there are pieces that no models can wear, so substitutions must be made. It's easy to destroy a card and add a new one.

It's easy to work out the lineup by arranging and rearranging the cards within a sequence until you are satisfied with the best possible mix. Lay them out on a table like a big game of solitaire and try different orders until you have the best. When each sequence has been lined up, number all of the cards in the upper right corner from 1 to the last number of the show.

Grouping the Merchandise

There is one more step after the cards are lined up and numbered before the show is ready to be fitted on the models. This is a dramatic grouping of the clothes, which is done for two reasons:

1. Bringing each model out singly, in a long continuous parade, lacks drama and excitement. The show is more interesting if the presentation is varied—sometimes single models, sometimes compatible groups.
2. You can make a stronger fashion statement by bringing out a group of models wearing versions of one fashion theme. An example is the pants fashion that emerged so strongly in 1968. By grouping six or eight pants outfits and bringing them all on stage at once, a strong belief in the fashion is imparted to the audience. In the same way, several fashions in one color combination, or with similar details, or with the same accessories are interesting when the models come out as a group.

Three young models wear variations of the uniform look in fashion, while the drummer and musical instruments accent the idea. Courtesy of *Seventeen* Magazine.

Go through the deck of cards once more and decide how to group the clothes so that the maximum drama is achieved. Fasten each of the groups with a paper clip.

The cards are now ready to be used for typing the lineup in list form, after which they may be used by the fashion director to write the commentary.

The lineup is usually typed on stencils so that it may be reproduced in quantity and distributed to the entire show staff. With an appropriate pen or stylus, draw brackets around each group of models who are to come out together (see illustration). Copies of this lineup will be used in the fittings and in the dressing room during the show. If it is a store show a copy should be sent to every buyer whose merchandise is being used. Check off her pieces so that the list may be posted in the stockroom for reference when customers inquire about the show fashions.

MODELS AND DRAMA

Models who are celebrities or special types can be used to glamorize a show. Yardley has used famous models Jean Shrimpton and Twiggy as

GROUP I -- THE COMMON DENOMINATORS (HE/SHE)

THEY GO 'TOGETHER'

   PLAIDS WITH PUNCH

   1. PENDLETON -- Black/white/red mammoth glen plaid wool suit: jacket with notch
       collar, cutaway front, pockets with flaps; matching skirt slightly A,
       taffeta lining.
       WITH:
       Claret red wool long-sleeved pullover turtleneck: cable bands down front.
       WITH:
       Matching black/white visor cap.

   2. PENDLETON -- Black/white/red mammoth glen plaid wool belted man's coat:
       black leather buttons, notch collar, straight sleeves with band through
       loops.
       WITH:
       Matching brushed wool blanket with fringed ends. (52" X 70")
       WITH:
       ESQUIRE SPORTSWEAR -- 100% cotton corduroy black men's pants with trim leg
       and western pockets. (HE)

   3. COUNTRY PLACE -- Brown glen plaid wool/cotton/rayon/10% other fibers cape;
       zip front; gold chains and buttons over zipper; stand-up collar; arm slashes;
       self scarf with fringed ends.

   4. COUNTRY PLACE -- Brown glen plaid wool/cotton/rayon/10% other fibers cape:
       pointed collar; tan leather buttons; arm slashes; long self scarf with fringe. (HE)

   PATTERNED PLAID PANT POW

   5. JUNIORITE -- Black with green/red/yellow overplaid turbo acrylic bonded
       jumpsuit: sleeveless; deep U-neck; small gold buttons down front; fake
       pocket flaps.
       WITH:
       Red orlon finely ribbed pullover: long sleeves; mock turtleneck.

   6. FOUR CORNERS -- Black/red tartan plaid bonded Creslan acrylic jumpsuit:
       sleeveless; high neck; low cut-out sides; side tab belts.
       WITH:
       Black Orlon acrylic finely ribbed pullover: long sleeves; mock turtleneck.

   7. LASSIE -- Red wool coachman's cape: pointed collar; epaulettes with silver
       buttons; silver buttons down front and on parenthesis pockets; arm slashes;
       with red/green/navy plaid acrylic long scarf with navy fringe.
       WITH:
       Red/green/navy wool/nylon/rayon bonded plaid pants.

   8. RIGAMAROLE -- Plum wool/20% other fibers melton pantsuit: coat has red/green/
       navy/plum plaid notch collar and facing; double-breasted with silver buttons;
       bellows-pleated pockets; red/green/navy/plum wool straight leg pants.

   TOOLING ALONG

   9. MAHARAJAH IMPORTS -- Peach color glace calf leather vest: collarless;
       concealed hook/eye closing; slashed at sides; square and round tooled
       medallion trim; pink satin lining.
       WITH:
       VAN HEUSEN 417 -- Orange/purple/white horizontal print on dark green ground
       cotton shirt: button-on white pique collar; short front placket; long sleeves.
       WITH:
       PAUL RESSLER -- Menswear striped wool/nylon/acrylic bonded to acetate boy-girl
       pants: cuffed wide leg; watch pockets.

First page of the lineup for a fashion show, typed from the merchandise cards and ready
to be used for fitting the models. Outfits that are to be shown together are bracketed.

stars of beauty shows. Young model Colleen Corby has provided star material for teen shows. "The March of Dimes" show was built around celebrity models.

As accents for an Oriental Festival, Macy's of Kansas City imported three top models from the Orient. Higbee's of Cleveland brought over the famous Italian men's tailor Brioni plus his leading male models. The men attending the show may not have cared, but the ladies certainly appreciated the treat.

Celebrity model Jean Shrimpton talks to the audience at a Yardley beauty show staged in cooperation with Higbee's of Cleveland. Courtesy of Yardley of London.

THE IMPORTANCE OF MUSIC

Music is almost as essential to a good fashion show as good fashions themselves. You can't stage an exciting show without it. Exceptions are informal modeling and small shows in a department of a store. However, it is always appropriate and helpful, no matter how small or informal the show:

- Good music is entertainment per se.
- Music can add emphasis to the different fashions that are shown if it is well programmed.
- Music helps the models to walk and dance.
- Music can span any lags in the show if models fail to appear on cue.
- Good music can cover up for any models who lack snap and spirit, giving the illusion that they are lively.
- People react to music, so that if it is good, they will react favorably to the show.

The Contribution of Live Music

The value of live music as opposed to tape or records is great. Live music has a vitality and resonance that is lacking in recordings. Also, musicians can "play it by ear" during the show and pace the music with the models. They can add a few bars if the sequence is lagging, or cut off a few if it is going fast. Be sure they are located so that they can see the stage and runway.

Live music can be programmed much more accurately and appropriately with the individual fashions and with the sequences. Although the purpose of music is to support the fashion story, a good music group can be an attraction that helps build the audience. A special number halfway through the show adds entertainment value and gives the show crew and models a welcome breather.

The psychological effect of a live music group is not to be underestimated. It implies something special and inspires a festive spirit.

The Tempo is the Test

Forrest Perrin, New York's best known director of fashion show music, maintains that a lively tempo is the secret of successful fashion-show music. This authority, who has played for so many models that they would probably circle the globe if lined up at one time, believes in playing twice as fast for a fashion show as for any other function. He says that the rhythm must be "driving" so that the models are forced to push themselves to keep up.

A rock group not only provides music for a young fashion show, but becomes the stage setting too. Courtesy of Higbee's, Cleveland.

This specialist also recommends changing the pace of the music by coming in with a different rhythm every two or three minutes, or even for every model if she is on the runway as long as fifty seconds. An alternate suggestion is to assign a tempo appropriate for the clothes in each grouping or scene of four or five minutes, but never longer. The tempo might vary from rock to bossa nova, to percussion, to waltz. Many contemporary shows, especially young shows, use only rock music. In this case, he advises using all of the best new numbers that have been recorded by the top stars.

These additional music tips are shared by Forrest Perrin:

1. When planning the music, plan the instruments accordingly. If the show has an Indian theme or sequence, a flute might be added; if Japanese, a gong could be effective; if Italian, a mandolin; or if Swiss, an accordion.

2. Arm yourself with a book of song titles as a reminder. There are many general books of titles, classified in every way you can imagine: by year, by show, by writer, by occasion, by country, by ethnic

group, by tempo, and so on. Whatever your need or type of show, check the book department of a good music store for an appropriate list. One good basic book is *The Variety Music Cavalcade* by Julius Mattfeld, which lists titles from 1620 to 1961.

3. Anyone who produces fashion shows regularly, or who provides music for shows, would find the time well spent to compile a set of reference notebooks of song titles. Classify by use: male music for male models, such as "Stout-Hearted Men"; children's music, such as "Who's Afraid of the Big Bad Wolf"; tunes for different countries, such as French, Greek, Indian; and so on.

The Technicalities of Recorded Music

If recorded music must be used for a fashion show, an especially made tape is best. However, this requires skill not only in the programming and cutting but also in the use. It has been done very successfully, but should not be attempted unless everyone involved is familiar with making and using tape.

Before making a tape, each sequence of the show must be timed as accurately as possible and the taped music or sound fitted into that time segment. Then the show must be thoroughly rehearsed to be sure the timing works out as planned. Even so, a model is always likely to have a last-minute emergency that delays the show, such as a broken zipper or a boot that won't come off. The operator who is handling the tape must be on the alert for such a hitch and be able to handle it. The starter who is pushing the models out, as well as the commentator (if any), must also be especially alert in synchronizing with the tape.

If the elements are not right for a special tape, a purchased tape of music may be used. Select one (or more) that is appropriate for the particular show and also rehearse the models with it. Otherwise, you may have music coming on that is quite inappropriate for the clothes on the runway.

The least desirable method of providing recorded music is a record player. The psychological effect on both audience and models is a negative one. It gives an amateurish impression of not having or knowing a more professional way. Then there is the tattletale time between each record as the player shifts from one to another.

If you must use a record player, try using two machines with a skillful operator, or two operators. In this way you can program a change of music pace for each sequence, and occasionally even for one group of clothes within a sequence. This requires a cued script for the operators of the record players.

How to Program the Music

Three considerations govern the best possible choice of the music to be used during a show:

1. Music must have pace and variety—fast and slow, loud and soft, lively and relaxed—keyed to the fashions.
2. The kind of music chosen should have appeal for the type of audience expected. A group of matrons would neither appreciate nor understand a rock group, but a young audience would. The adult group would be more likely to enjoy popular show tunes.
3. The kind of musicians should be compatible for the kind of show. One organist can be effective for a bridal show, or a pianist for a children's show, for example.

So that the music director or group leader can have as much time as possible to program the music in an interesting way, give him a lineup of the entire show when it is ready. He needs to know the themes of the sequences, how many models or outfits appear in each, and brief descriptions of the individual fashions. He can then select the appropriate music for each segment, estimate how many minutes he needs to fill in each sequence, as well as choose music that complements the specific clothes. If the musicians have not played for a fashion show before, they should be cautioned to select music that is easy to walk to with a snappy step. They should also be cued to play softly while the commentator is talking.

An audience of high school or college age likes music in its own idiom, usually rock or a variation. This may be easier to dance to than walk to. Thus many shows are staged entirely in dancing, with the models dancing down the runway singly, or in group routines, or with the opposite sex. A blending of all three makes for the most interest. This inspires a lively show and adds movement to the clothes.

PURE ENTERTAINMENT—OR NOT

The question of how much and what kind of entertainment, if any, should be included in a fashion show is answered by the one word "appropriateness." Good entertainment (and don't make any concessions to less than good) in the right amount will add to any fashion show. The amount varies with the type of show, the purpose, and the audience:

- If you are trying to sell directly by the show, let the entertainment be an exciting foil that sets off the clothes and makes them more appealing to the audience. Don't have so much entertainment that the drama of the clothes is completely lost or buried.

- If the show is for the press, remember that they are on the job, their time is limited, that they are a very sophisticated audience — and that they are there for news. Everyone is out to impress them. So make any entertainment short, sweet, and the best. Otherwise, it is advisable to eliminate it.

- If the show is a trade or professional one, be guided by the time the audience can devote to it. During business hours, make the entertainment a short punctuation mark, or eliminate it entirely. At a social function outside of business hours, the pace may be more relaxed and the type of entertainment more varied. Also, it may be an "in" type of entertainment. For example, the book of the Milliken Breakfast Show is always a retailer-manufacturer story with many lines in the idiom that would be understood or appreciated only by such an audience.

- If the fashion show is purely for entertainment, as at a benefit or other social function, go all out on the entertainment and let the clothes become subordinate (although they should be chosen for their entertainment value too). Good public relations and publicity will accrue to the lender of the fashions and thus indirect (instead of direct) sales will result as their payment.

Choosing the Entertainment

Almost any kind of entertainment that teams happily with audience and clothes can be used in a fashion show:

- Music by the group booked for the show is the most obvious. A good group can play a short overture, and also have five to ten minutes midway in the show for a "concert" number. A good vocalist with the group may provide the entertainment.

- Famous stars may sometimes be obtained to perform at a show for the benefit of a national charity. An example is the "March of Dimes" shows where stars such as Danny Kaye appeared.

- A featured vocalist or singing group may be booked. Be sure to check whether they can and will perform with the musicians who will play for the models. You would be put to considerable additional expense if special musicians are necessary to accompany special artists.

A tap-dancing group relates fashions inspired by the 1930s to the period in a snappy fashion show produced by Abraham & Straus of Brooklyn.

"The Wheels of Fashion" show produced by Morgan's of Montreal, Quebec, Canada, inspires the easy-to-do backdrop and the models' dance.

- Special entertainers can point up certain fashions. A cowboy with rope tricks, a cowboy singer, or a square dance group are amusing to introduce western-inspired fashions. A magician can make a strong point of the magic of sportswear separates.
- A good dancer is a pleasure to see, but must be of professional caliber. Beware of dancing-school amateurs. The type of dancing must fit in with the show. A ballet dancer might be charming at a children's show, but poison at a teens' show.
- A fashion show can be staged as a musical or even a play. However, this is the most difficult kind of show to produce unless professionals are available for writing the script and music. The Milliken show is produced by a sizable staff of persons experienced in the theater with the entire cast drawn from Broadway actors, singers, dancers.
- Films or slides are a fairly recent innovation in fashion shows. Especially programmed slides, movie clips, or abstract images, usually accompanied by appropriate sound or music, is a contemporary means of adding entertainment.

Programming the Entertainment

Special entertainment has to be programmed so that it becomes an integral part of the fashion show and does not overpower the fashions. There are four ways to ensure the appropriate use of entertainment:

1. Musical numbers that are not actually integrated into the show but are provided by the musicians booked to play the show. The fact that it is the same musicians provides the continuity.
2. Any entertainers become an integral part of the show if their act relates in some way to the fashions, for example, a cowboy singer who relates to western fashions.
3. Each sequence of the show may be introduced with entertainment that in some way relates to the group of fashions. This is the format followed in the "March of Dimes" fashion show when entertainment by a celebrity was employed to introduce the scenes such as a short ballet based on the fashion theme of the scene.
4. A musical or play melds fashions and entertainment by virtue of its form.

PLANNING THE SETTINGS AND PROPS FOR DRAMA

The current trend in the theater, television, and fashion shows is toward settings in stark simplicity. Stylized shapes, forms, platforms, cubes, steps, and the like are used with dramatic effect to set off the performers. Although it would be boring if every show were presented in this way, the trend does influence the look you want to achieve on stage.

The least-cluttered appearance is the most effective as a background for fashion shows. In the theater a lavish or a "busy" set can complement and enhance the actors who have lines and action to help keep them from being overpowered. In a fashion show the silent model and clothes can easily be lost against such a set. The model needs something that allows action so that she can show movement of the clothes, such as steps or platforms or doors. The signature of Walter Hazeltine who has staged the New York Fashion Group shows for many years is a series of doors, windows, or screens through which models move onto the stage.

In planning the background for the stage, try to relate it to the kind of show and audience. Certainly a different feeling should be projected for children's, teens', bridal, men's, couture, and so on. A children's show

A stretch screen with cavelike opening in center becomes a dramatic stage setting for *Seventeen* Magazine's "Experience" in the Waldorf-Astoria Grand Ballroom. Models poured through the opening while projection of slides and film played over the screen.

A group of models dance out of the giant stretch screen at the "Experience" fashion show staged by *Seventeen* Magazine.

setting may be amusing and colorful, teens may be snappy, bridal romantic, men's sporty, and couture elegant, to cite several examples.

Projection of slides and movie film has been used effectively on one or more screens as the only background for fashion presentations. This is especially appropriate for teens, since they are film-oriented. The big

Photographs of London scenes are enlarged as background stage setting for a "Young London Look Show." Courtesy of Michael Whittaker of London.

(a)

(b)

This group of photographs illustrates how Abraham & Straus wheeled in sets to change the scenes during their "The On Set" fashion show at The Brooklyn Academy of Music: (a) a compact foreign car transports "Between the Half Boosters;" (b) "Book Worms in Camel and Blue;" (c) "Long and Lovelies;" (d) "The Gray Society."

Projection of slides on a center screen adds drama and emphasis to the fashions modeled in *Seventeen* Magazine's "The Young Expressionists" fashion show.

problem in using projection is to be able to light the fashions without washing out the image on the screen. The secret is to keep models as far in front of the screen as possible, to light them from the wings while they are on stage if at all possible, and to keep follow spots focused on the runway. Lights focused from height down on the models is another solution.

Keep Props to a Minimum

The day of every model's carrying a prop in her hand to emphasize what she is wearing is past. Models should be so beautifully dressed and accessorized that the clothes speak for themselves and become an object lesson in fashion for the audience.

A racquet with a tennis dress or a club with a golf outfit is a natural, since these clothes have limited accessories and are fairly classic. The swing of a racquet or club gives the model some action for this kind of action sportswear. However, it isn't necessary to have a model carry a notebook or an apple to indicate that she is wearing a school outfit. It would be more attractive—and more profitable—to give her an appropriate school handbag.

Action props such as bicycles, motorcycles, or skates can add to a show, as evidenced by the shows on wheels and the show on ice skates. Whenever any apparatus with a motor is brought inside a building, check the fire laws on whether the motor may be started or whether all gasoline must be drained.

THE DRAMA OF LIGHTING

Aside from the fact that good lighting is a requisite for showing clothes, it can add drama to the show. UV (ultraviolet) and strobe lighting are effective gimmicks to use occasionally. UV lighting permits certain items or parts of the fashion figure to be seen on a dark stage in white or glowing color. One show opened the curtain on a row of models swinging out toward the audience. Only the swings and soles of the models' shoes could be seen. When the stage lights went up in several

These models carried sports equipment but didn't move in Filene's and *Life* Magazine's "This is the Life" fashion show in Boston to highlight clothes and activities for expanded leisure hours. Each girl posed on a small platform that revolved on a mechanical track.

seconds, the surprised audience applauded the row of beautifully dressed models. This involved the use of iridescent paint on the swings and soles of the shoes (purchased from a scenic house or art supply store) and UV lighting.

Strobe lights can impart a mechanical look to models, dancers, or musicians. A little of this goes a long way because it is hard to look at. Just a few seconds can be dramatic.

The newest use of lighting as a part of the show is the light show accompanied by sound. The first light shows featured bee lights that were programmed to dance to sound. They might be in rows surrounding doors or screens on the stage, or might dot some image on the backdrop. The light show next evolved into lights and images projected onto a screen with a sound accompaniment. Even though rear projection is used, there is the problem of lighting the models without losing the images on the screen, as was mentioned in the preceding section.

Attractive effects may be achieved by the use of colored gels over the spotlights. A lighting specialist can supply many other good ideas if he is brought into the planning at an early stage. He must be cautioned, however, to remember that the fashions are the stars.

Focus on the Clothes

The lighting of the clothes must never be overlooked. Paul Saitta, a lighting specialist for major network television shows and the head of Vega Associates, theatrical consultants, advises anyone producing a fashion show to bear in mind these points:

- Be sure to provide sufficient time before and after the show for loading the lighting equipment in and out, and for setting it up and focusing spotlights.
- White lighting is the best to show off the clothes.
- The biggest problem in lighting fashions is to keep from blinding the audience with the spotlights, especially the follow spots. There is no way to eliminate this, so efforts should be made to minimize it. Locate spotlights as high as possible so that they focus down on the models. A balcony or ballroom tier is a good place for them. This will "spot" the clothes much better than lights placed on the same level as the runway or models. Low-placed lights are more likely to blind the audience.
- All stationary spotlights must be carefully focused before the show begins. This is a tedious job if a large number of lights are used, so adequate time must be allowed.

- Specific instructions must be given to the operators of the follow spots. Each man needs to know at which point he picks up a model with his light, and where he drops her. These operators should be rehearsed with the models, especially at the dress rehearsal.

THE SHAPE OF THE RUNWAY ADDS SHOWMANSHIP

Even the way the runway is designed and set up can add interest and excitement to the staging. Some of these ways are:

> straight out from the stage
> zig-zag shape
> T-shape
> U-shape (passerelle)
> with platform at end for turns

A straight runway extending from the stage is the least exciting. A zig-zag runway is simple, yet gives a more interesting look to the mod-

The shape of the runway offers a way of adding movement and variety. This symmetrical cross-shaped runway forms a dignified means of showing designer fashions. Courtesy of Jordan Marsh of Boston.

A runway traced in footlights zigzags through the audience at a designer fashion show staged with an oriental theme, by Filene's of Boston.

Models kick to show off leather shorts on an unusual runway formed by a platform running from door to wing of a jet plane at Titche's show in a hanger.

A teen fashion show staged in-the-round on a platform constructed in the center of Higbee's auditorium, Cleveland. Models move in and out of the abstract shapes that form the set.

Models skip rope on the in-the-round "The Thing Is . . ." show sponsored by Higbee's of Cleveland.

eling as the girls walk first one way and then aother. The passerelle runway as used in the staging of the musical "Hello Dolly" is effective. This shape is conducive to routines and to interesting movement of the models. The musicians can be placed in the center to utilize that space. A straight extension can be added to the passerelle if the room is large enough.

A fashion show in the round is achieved via a runway in the center of the room. This may be any shape, such as a square, an X, or a Y. Two sets of steps enable models to enter at one point and exit at another, or entries and exits may be varied.

8

The Dressing Room and its Staff

For tight control of a good show, one large dressing room for all models is desirable in spite of the fact that it may look like organized confusion. When the whole dressing operation is concentrated, fewer people are required and better organization is actually possible. It should be on the same level as the stage or runway and as near as possible.

In laying out the dressing room, traffic patterns are essential. Strive for:

- The most efficient pattern of exits and entrances.
- A minimum of running around by the models.
- Elimination of bottlenecks.
- Ramps instead of steps in or out of the room, if any.
- Models' dressing areas spaced to avoid crowding.

The floor plan illustrated is an ideal layout for twenty models and eighty outfits. It may be scaled down or up as the occasion requires. Note that models exit near the entrance to the stage and enter near the end of the runway.

Each model has a chair for putting on makeup, stockings, and shoes. Stations that a model may or may not have occasion to use—accessories, hairdresser, makeup artist—are out of the general line of traffic. The presser is also out of the way, as is the water and coffee table.

EQUIPMENT FOR THE DRESSING ROOM

Certain equipment is essential for the dressing room. Compromises or concessions where these necessities are concerned only lead to disappointing results. The models are the stars, so they should have everything they need to do a good job.

145

A dressing room may be set up anywhere when a show goes "on location." It's the cabin of a jet plane for this show given in an airline hanger by Titche's of Dallas. Clothes were hooked over the overhead shelf.

Dressing Tables, Mirrors, Chairs

To do her work, each model requires a work area. Her own dressing table for makeup and hair paraphernalia is desirable. It need only be a small table with a mirror. (The tiny cocktail tables that hotels have are fine.) The popular makeup mirrors with one side magnified and lights around the frame are best if you have enough electrical outlets.

If there are not enough dressing tables available, rows of tables with makeup mirrors and chairs can be placed so that access is easy for all models to take their turns.

Several full-length mirrors should be spaced throughout the room so that models may take a look at the whole outfit after they are dressed, and check for any dangling threads, undergear, or tags.

Racks for Clothes

The only practical racks for the clothes are pipe racks with rollers or casters. These may be rented. Check the yellow pages of the telephone directory under these headings: "Rack Rental—Hat and Coat," "Check Room Equipment Renting," or "Party Supplies—Retail and Rental."

If a rental service is not available in your city, perhaps a local department store would lend or rent racks. If it is a store show, the clothes will probably be delivered to the scene of the show on pipe racks. However, they may be crowded on the racks so that additional ones are required.

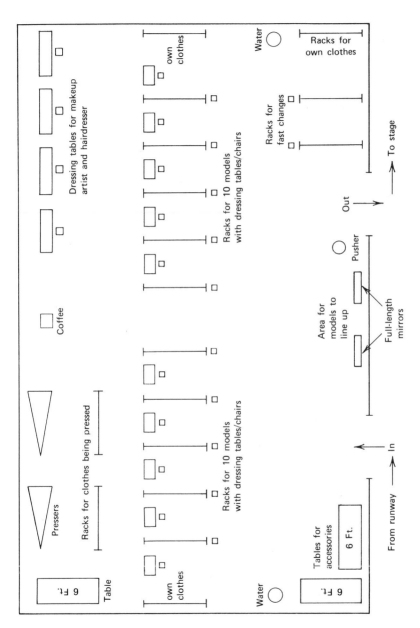

Floor plan for a dressing room, laid out for about twenty models and eighty outfits.

Dressing rooms have always been crowded and busy. Here, models and celebrities sip coffee as they make up at rows of tables and mirrors before one of the early "March of Dimes" fashion shows. Courtesy of The National Foundation—March of Dimes.

Models for an early "March of Dimes" fashion show keep busy while waiting to dress. Courtesy of The National Foundation—March of Dimes.

Don't accept racks that have hooks for the clothes like those used in many checkrooms, or those that have attached hangers. The former are completely impractical, while the latter are awkward to use since the hangers cannot be removed.

ORGANIZING THE MERCHANDISE

There are two ways in which the clothes that each model will show may be arranged in the dressing room:

1. By Model

If a model has more than two outfits to wear, the most efficient way to arrange her clothes is to assemble them all together on one rack in one place. Two models can easily use one rack. It is possible but not convenient for three of four to use one rack if it isn't too crowded and there is room for dividers.

If two models use one rack, arrange one girl's clothes at the front of the rack in order of appearance and the other model's at the back in order. A big sheet of paper or cardboard clipped onto a skirt hanger in the middle of the rack will keep the clothes from getting mixed up in the rush of changing.

At the end of each rack, use cellophane or masking tape to attach a big sheet of drawing paper for each model with her name, her numbers in the lineup, and identifying descriptions of her outfits. If more than one model uses the rack, attach the sheets one above the other, or one at each end if the rack is arranged so that the girls can work from both ends. One alternative is to use these sheets as dividers in front of each girl's clothes. Use felt markers for lettering the information in a size easily seen:

MARY WHITE

3 — Red Suit, White Sweater

14 — Navy Sailor Outfit

30 — White Crepe Cocktail

42 — Pink Chiffon Formal

The accessory bags should be hooked over the hangers with the clothes or placed on separate hangers and hung behind each outfit, so that the model can easily arrange them after she arrives. Any small props may be placed in the bags, such as a tennis racquet or golf club, or laid on the floor under the rack. Large props belong on a prop table under the supervision of someone with a lineup who can hand them to the models as they need them.

2. By Order of Lineup

If each model wears only one or two outfits, all of the clothes may be arranged on racks in numerical order, with lineups posted in several prominent places so each model knows her number or numbers. Each rack may have posted on sheets of drawing paper the number of outfits on that rack with the models' names. Each hanger should carry a tag with the number of the outfit.

RACK 1
1 — Mary White — White Pant Suit
2 — June Zale — Navy/White Pant Suit
3 — Suzie Smith — Red Pant Suit
4 — Linda Malone — White Top, Black Pants
5 — Kathy Jones — Black Pant Suit, White Scarf
6 — Sunnie Simon — Black Jersey Dress, Red Trim
7 — Nancy Hale — Black Jersey Dress, Gold Trim
8 — Joan Miller — Black Jersey Jumpsuit
9 — Sara Winston — Red Sweater, Black Skirt
10 — Salli Potter — Red Shirt, Black Tweed Skirt

ACCESSORY TABLES

Even though each outfit has been completely accessorized, it's a good idea to have a few extra accessories on hand for an emergency. Something may get lost, torn, or broken and have to be replaced at the last minute. Or an outfit may have to be fitted on a different model, requiring different accessories. Hosiery is always likely to be torn.

Arrange the spare accessories in an orderly fashion on one or more tables with at least one person in charge to assist the models. The following would make up an adequate assortment:

- *Headgear.* Types should be supplied for whatever merchandise is being used in the show. For example, if showing coats and suits, have on hand a few extra hats that will go with these, and so on for dresses and whatever else you are showing.
- *Scarfs.* A small assortment of types, colors, and patterns.

- *Jewelry.* A few pieces of tailored jewelry, dressy cocktail, and formal evening. Be guided by the current fashion trends.
- *Handbags.* This accessory is not essential. However, a bag does complete an outfit and should be used when it doesn't hide or interfere with the modeling. Several handbags in the key accessory colors and in the leading types will suffice.
- *Gloves.* A few pairs in basic neutral colors, in several lengths.
- *Hosiery.* Be sure to have extra stockings on hand in basic colors or in any important colors that are being used in the show. These may be stretch stockings that fit all. If socks or any other types of hosiery are being shown, provide extras.
- *Shoes.* This presents a problem because of fit. However, professional models are used to walking down a runway in a misfit if absolutely necessary. Toes may be stuffed with tissue or a wad of plastic wrap. Also, models can sometimes arrange to exchange shoes, or use the same ones. If possible, you might have on hand daytime and streetwear types, dressy and evening shoes—if you are showing clothes in these categories.

Children's Accessories

In a children's fashion show, sizes are likely to vary so much that it would be difficult to provide extra accessories. Care should be taken when fitting that each little model has everything she needs. A child is so appealing on the runway that she (or he) doesn't need props.

Men's Accessories

A few extra ties, ascots, and scarfs should be on hand. Black stretch socks are a good spare investment. Otherwise, at the time of fitting be sure each model has everything he needs to complete his look.

Emergency Supplies

Gather together any group of people and emergencies are sure to arise. Models are no different. Thus it pays to keep a kit of emergency supplies in the dressing room during a show for the models and others working in the room. If you do shows regularly, just pack a basic box and always have it on hand. These are the usual necessities:

aspirin	clothes brush and lint remover
Band-Aids	colorless nail enamel for stopping
bobby pins, hairpins	runs
cellophane tape	cotton

deodorants
drawing paper for marking racks
dress shields (may be paper)
emery board, nail file
extension cords
felt markers
flashlight
hair spray
head masks
masking tape, one to two-inch
mints, hard candies
nail polish and remover
needles
paper clips
pencils, pens
pin cushions

rubber bands, thin and heavier
rubber cement
safety pins, straight pins, hat pins
sanitary napkins, tampons
scissors
shoe horns
shoe fillers (tissue or thin plastic)
smelling salts
spot remover
stapler
string
tape measures
thread in basic colors
tissues
tissue paper

POSTING THE LINEUP

Everyone in the dressing room needs easy access to the lineup. Therefore, it should be posted in several key spots in the room as well as by the door where models line up before going on stage and by the door where they return to the dressing room. It is desirable to post the show in two ways in order to save time and questions.

1. The essential way to post the show is the lineup of outfits in numerical order, by scenes or sequences.
2. An additional aid is a list of the models in alphabetical order. Under each one's name should be her numbers and outfits in the show. This type of list is necessary if the clothes are arranged in the dressing room in numerical order instead of by model. Otherwise models may lose time in trying to find their numbers and outfits.

THE STAFF BEHIND THE SCENES

While the models may be the stars of the show, the dressing room workers are the supporting cast without which a show just can't succeed.

Dressers

There should be a dresser for every model in a large show. In a smaller show, a dresser may be able to handle two or, at most, three models. The ideal dresser is organized, calm, fast—and tall. It is always difficult to find women for this most unglamourous of jobs. One store solved the problem by training a group of freelance women who work by the hour. The required number are called in for each show and work from the time the clothes are pulled from the departments until they are returned. They know store policies and so may be trusted with detaching tags and retagging, taping shoes, doing touchup pressing, and making minor repairs or alterations. By showtime, they know the clothes as well as anyone and are able to dress the models with skill and speed.

Each dresser should go through the outfits with her model or models before the show. If she has any questions about how a model wants to put on certain things, this is the time to ask. Dressers should unzip and unfasten the clothes as the model wishes. Accessories and pieces should be checked to see that nothing is missing. Any loose buttons or other minor repairs should be taken immediately to the alteration hand.

Dressing the model for her first appearance is easy, but changes are difficult because there are usually only several minutes between numbers. When the model goes on stage, the dresser should prepare for her return: be ready to help her get out of the clothes she is wearing, especially something difficult like boots; have the next outfit off the hanger and ready to put on in order; even be ready to get on her knees to help with shoes and boots; and give a quick check for the overall look (no open zippers, no embarrassing droopy stockings or dangling underwear). Hosiery may sometimes be worn in layers and peeled off with changes.

As the model returns to the runway, the dresser should quickly hang up the clothes that have just been shown and get the next outfit ready. At the end of the show, she should not leave until she and the model have put all clothes back on hangers, accessories in bags, and possibly shoes in boxes.

Pusher

The pusher (or pushers) holds a lineup and rounds up the models from their dressing areas. If one is missing from the lineup, she finds her and does whatever is necessary to get her ready and in place.

The pusher should know all of the models by name and by sight. Thus it should be someone who works with them regularly.

Checker

Unless someone who knows fashion and the clothes checks each model before she leaves the dressing room, embarrassing moments can occur. Someone who has helped in the fittings is especially qualified to handle this spot.

The checker, equipped with a lineup, stations herself in the lineup area after making sure that her list is corrected with all last-minute changes. She must give a quick once-over look at each model—from hair and makeup to shoes. She instructs the model about any necessary changes or repairs to achieve a perfect total look, and never permits a model to leave the room with chewing gum in her mouth.

In a big show, two checkers should be on hand in order not to hold up the show.

Starter

This is probably the most crucial member of the dressing room staff for it is her responsibility to start each model on cue at the right moment.

The starter has to rehearse thoroughly with the whole fashion-show company. Impact can be totally lost if a model comes out too soon or too late. The starter must know the cues and meet them with split-second timing. She is armed with a complete script on a clipboard (attach a pencil or pen for any last-minute changes).

Makeup Artist

A representative of a cosmetic company or someone from a store's cosmetic department should have a convenient station for making up the models. This is not essential if the models are professionals and experienced in runway makeup. If nonprofessionals are modeling, they need help. Show makeup must be a little more colorful because the strong lights wash out a percentage of the color. Also, makeup colors should be appropriate for wearing in artificial light (not change color).

Place the makeup area in a spot easily accessible to all models—yet not in a line of traffic (see diagram). He or she needs a table with mirror and a chair or stool for the model.

Hairdresser

The comments about makeup in the preceding section apply to a hairdresser. See diagram for placement in the room.

Hair styles must be appropriate for the clothes worn. Wigs and hairpieces solve the problem of changing from daytime clothes to evening. Professional models have their own hairpieces that are appropriate for them. However, it's a good idea to have a varied supply on hand—or these may be selected for the individual models at the time of the fittings.

Alteration Hand

No matter how well the show has been fitted, there is always a need for an alteration hand or a seamstress in the dressing room to make a quick repair or unstick a zipper. Also, there is always a model who calls in sick at the last minute and her clothes must be fitted on another model (or dropped). This may mean a quick hem change or a tuck here or there. Appropriate equipment is needed.

This helper may also be able to handle pressing (see next section).

Pressers

It's a rare show that doesn't need last-minute pressing. Every wrinkle must be eliminated so that clothes appear on the runway as if they had just "stepped out of a bandbox."

Depending on the size of the show, one or two pressers are needed. This can be a presser from the alteration department of the store providing the clothes; a presser from a maid service (available in large cities); someone's maid borrowed from home; or a member of the fashion-show staff. (Neophytes in the fashion business are frequently surprised at how unglamorous some of the tasks turn out to be!)

Remember to check the equipment the pressers need: ironing boards with clean cloth, steam-and-dry iron, clean pressing cloths. Some hotels have boards and irons available, but you must provide the pressing cloths.

Protection

In a dressing room filled with expensive merchandise and many people, professional protection is essential. Otherwise there will be losses and thefts. This is discussed in detail in Chapter 12.

WHEN SHOULD MODELS AND STAFF ARRIVE?

Half an hour before show time is just about right for the models' arrival. Any more time than this causes confusion and fatigue. Also, they tend to wander away and get lost if there is too much time. On the other hand, they must have adequate time to:

> go over clothes with dresser
> put on makeup
> comb hair
> handle any emergency
> dress in first outfit

If special makeup is being applied and a hairdresser is styling the hair, more time is needed and models should arrive forty-five minutes to an hour ahead of curtain time.

Other workers in the dressing room should be there and have everything set up and organized before any models appear. The amount of time needed depends on the particular job and the size of the show— forty-five minutes to an hour before the curtain.

FACILITIES FOR MODELS AND STAFF

Models and staff members need a place to put their personal belongings—hats, coats, umbrellas, and especially handbags and personal jewelry. The ideal arrangement is to have a separate rack and area where they may put their outer wear. To avoid mixups and losses, it is best to have an attendant take care of this rack and give out checks.

Handbags and personal jewelry are a big problem in the dressing room, even though there is a guard on duty. A reliable and responsible person should be in charge of checking these and watching them throughout the entire show. Most models know that it is unwise to bring very much money, but nonprofessionals and staff should be cautioned about this and other valuables.

The Staff Needs Sustenance

There's something about the excitement and tension of a fashion show that turns models and staff into compulsive eaters and drinkers. So preparation must be made.

Packaged mints and some hard candies are good to have on hand. Pitchers of ice water and glasses are essential. If drinking fountains are used, provide paper cups so clothes won't be splattered. Never have chewing gum around nor permit models to chew.

Although eating in a dressing room is a nuisance and may soil clothes, sometimes it is necessary, depending on the time of the show. If it is a breakfast show and models report early, have coffee and small rolls in the dressing room. If models must be fed at lunch, serve only sandwiches, coffee, and soft drinks. If it is a dinner show, try to book models to arrive after dinner and have on hand only coffee and water.

Never serve alcoholic beverages to models and staff, nor permit them to order these. The only exception is one glass of champagne if you wish to be very gala, glamorous, and generous. It gives the models a special feeling and sparkle. (Mary Quant and Lester Gaba recommend this.)

Smoking is a serious dressing-room problem. It must be unequivocally prohibited for everyone because it is too dangerous.

9

Be Kind to the Merchandise

The heart of a fashion show is the mechandise that the models wear — all of the clothes and accessories. It must be handled a great deal during the course of preparation for a show, the show itself, and the cleanup afterward.

Handling the merchandise is like handling money. In most cases, it must survive the show in a condition that enables it to be sold later. This means tender loving care at all stages.

Since most shows are staged for the purpose of selling and promoting, some markdowns can be justified as promotion expense. However, these should be kept to a minimum. It is better to have no markdowns at all.

When clothes are borrowed from a designer, a couture house, or a manufacturer, sizable sums of money are involved because original samples are costly. One piece can run into hundreds, or even thousands, of dollars. He may not have to sell it after the show, but he needs it as a part of his collection.

Suggestions on how models can help care for the clothes are given in Chapter 10. This chapter deals with how the show staff itself can prevent needless damage and losses. Much of this information relates directly to retail stores because they handle more clothes for shows than anyone else. However, the principles may be applied to handling merchandise for any fashion show.

CHECKING MERCHANDISE OUT OF STOCK IN A STORE

Large stores have forms and procedures for taking merchandise out of stock for show purposes and returning it. The fashion director and her assistants are obligated to follow the procedure to the letter. Shortages

D. H. HOLMES CO., LTD.

MERCHANDISE LOAN

D. H. HOLMES CO., LTD.

MERCHANDISE LOAN

D. H. HOLMES CO., LTD.

MERCHANDISE LOAN

DATE   DEPT.   STORE

Authorized By   Reason

(   )   (   )

Mdse. Will Be At   Period Required

(   )   (   )

QTY.	DESCRIPTION OF MDSE.	SERIAL NO.	RETAIL

Received By (   )   Dept. (   )

Returned Mdse. Rec'd. By (   ) Date (   )

White Copy   -   Goes with mdse. on loan   5102
Yellow Copy -   Receipt when mdse. returned
Blue Copy   -   Dept.

Merchandise loan form, in triplicate, used by D. H. Holmes of New Orleans.

are a major problem in stores so every effort is exerted to keep track of the borrowed merchandise and have it returned promptly to stock.

Usually the fashion director keeps a Loan Book or Transfer Book of forms for charging out merchandise (see example). It may be the same as the one that the display department uses. A form is completed in

Loan form used by Hutzler's of Baltimore when merchandise is taken out of stock for show purposes.

Compact loan form used by Hochschild, Kohn of Baltimore.

duplicate for each piece, listing style number, size, color, and price. One copy is left with the buyer who authorizes the loan to account for the garment, while the other is left in the book as a record for the fashion department.

Since stores frequently tour their fashion shows to their branches and occasionally send them to television stations, there are further formalities when merchandise is taken out of the store. The form used by one store shows the care taken to keep track of merchandise (see illustration). It is completed in triplicate, with the driver carrying one copy as his receipt. A copy may also be given to the protection department who may want to check it against the merchandise actually leaving the main store.

When the merchandise is returned to stock, it is signed for by the buyer or other authorized person as received in salable condition (the fashion department may be charged for damages or losses). The buyer's form may be retrieved by the fashion department or kept by the buyer as a reminder in answering customer inquiries about show merchandise.

FORM 6312 - JAN. 62   HOLMES

INTER-STORE TRIP SHEET   **5111**

FORM 6312 - JAN. 62   HOLMES

INTER-STORE TRIP SHEET   **5111**

FORM 6312 - JAN. 62   HOLMES

INTER-STORE TRIP SHEET   **5111**

DATE		TIME		ORIGINATED BY		

TO:

☐ CANAL ST.	☐ DELMONT
☐ LAKESIDE	☐ BON MARCHE
☐ DOWNTOWN	☐

FROM:

☐ CANAL ST.	☐ DELMONT
☐ LAKESIDE	☐ BON MARCHE
☐ DOWNTOWN	☐

SENT BY   ☐ OUR TRUCK   ☐ LIMOUSINE   ☐ BUS   ☐ PERSON

DEPT. NO.	ORDER NO. TRANSFER NO.	BULK DOLLEY NO.	UNITS OR PACKAGES	SEAL NO.	( ) OR EXCEPTION	RECEIVING DEPT. SIGNATURE

DRIVER	DATE	RECEIVING STORE	DATE
DRIVER	DATE	RECEIVING STORE	DATE

Sender prepares triplicate set for each point transferred to, keep pink copy and release white and yellow copies to driver, upon delivery driver leaves yellow copy, gets white copy receipted and returns it to sender.

Form used by D. H. Holmes of New Orleans when show merchandise travels from one store to another.

An alternate method is for each department that participates in shows to keep its own Loan Book. The fashion director signs the sheet when the merchandise is removed from the department and is given a copy. This accomplishes the same result and may be more efficient. In this way, each buyer has her records together in a book, while the fashion department may file the loose slips by classification for ease of reference.

Another method, less efficient, is to post in each department a list of merchandise taken out for a show. The pieces are crossed off as returned. Although this gives everyone in the department an easily visible list of out-merchandise, errors and losses can occur between the time the merchandise is physically removed and the list is compiled and posted. Also, a list on a wall is not the safest means of keeping a record.

FRAGILE—HANDLE WITH CARE

When the merchandise arrives in the fitting room, hang it on racks until the lineup is made and it is arranged in order. Be sure each hanger is right for the piece it supports. Clothes can easily be damaged or misshaped when hung on improper hangers. It is an economy to buy good hangers.

Leave enough space on each rack for the clothes to "breathe." Never crowd them to the point of crushing them and making them difficult to remove or replace on the rack.

Show merchandise must always be under lock and key when unattended.

The Little Things that Count

Clothes are like anything else—they can get out of working order when parts are damaged or lost. Zippers require careful handling to prevent jamming, tangling with fabric, tearing, or jumping the track. Loose buttons will be lost unless a stitch is taken in time.

Belts, scarfs, and other separate pieces that belong to a dress or outfit are easily lost unless they are attached to the garment during preparations for the show. A good model will reattach them after the show. However, a check of the merchandise after the show and before removing it from the dressing room will save many garments. It's easier to find missing parts at this time than it is to try to trace them later.

Accessories are easily lost (or stolen). If they have been bagged for each outfit, dressers or models are responsible for returning these to the

MANF.	STYLE NO.	COLOR	SIZE	DESCRIPTION	PRICE

MERCHANDISE USED IN FASHION SHOW   DEPT.

DAY AND DATE: PLACE:

TIME:
DATE PULLED: DATE RET'D:

Form appropriate for posting in department to list merchandise modeled in a fashion show.

bags. However, in making quick changes, it is sometimes impossible to do it immediately. By the end of the show, anything can have been lost in the confusion.

If models are accessorized from tables after they are dressed, their accessories should be taken from them as they return to the dressing room. Two assistants stationed at the door can quickly take everything but shoes and hosiery.

Keeping Shoes like New

Shoes are the one major item that cannot be sold as new after a fashion show unless special care is taken to protect them. Some fashion directors of stores, magazines, or manufacturers have wardrobes of shoes that are used only for shows or for publicity photographs. However, whenever shoes are borrowed from a shoe department or store, they must later be put back in stock and sold as new. When this is the case, several steps must be taken:

- Keep the shoes in their boxes when they are not being used. The box can be put into the model's accessory bag.
- Have the models wear them as briefly as possible to prevent stretching or getting out of shape, and to prevent perspiration stains inside.
- To keep the soles unmarred, cover them with one or two layers of masking tape obtained from an art store. Trim the tape around the

Fashion show staff taping the soles of shoes at the American Airlines hanger in Dallas before Titche's "The Out of Sight Flight" show with a jet plane as background.

edges, taking great care not to nick the soles. The tape can be easily peeled off after use without harming the soles (peel slowly).

• Return the shoes to the boxes after the show, checking the number and size beforehand to be sure they get back into the right boxes.

Tickets and Tags

No model must ever go on a runway with a hangtag or a price ticket showing. The best procedure from the standpoint of appearance is to remove all tags and tickets so that there is no chance of having one suddenly dangle.

Most stores remove fabric and fiber hangtags, but do not want price tags removed because of the trouble of reticketing afterward. In this case, the model or dresser is usually responsible for tucking these inside the garment and pinning, clipping, or taping them so that they will not fall out. Many tags are now computerized and these must never be pinned or mutilated. One fashion director has the models wear a rubber band on the arm under which tickets are tucked. This, of course, doesn't work with sheer fabrics.

Tags on accessories, such as jewelry, usually have to be removed. It is better to let the department take them off and preserve them in an envelope in order to replace them after the show. Or tags may be pinned to the Loan Sheet for easy and quick identification when being put back in stock.

Many price tags are attached with a plastic string and anchor so that they cannot be replaced after removal (to keep customers from wearing and returning clothes). Any garments ticketed this way have to go to the marking room to be reticketed unless the department has its own machine.

PRESSING BEFORE THE SHOW

A department store usually handles the pressing in the alteration department before delivering the clothes to the dressing room or scene of the show. Any other show will find it worth the expense to employ professional pressers, obtained from a maid service or a union, because they know how to protect merchandise from scorching, glazing, or other damage.

Any hems that have been changed or other temporary alterations that have been made are left unpressed or are only slightly pressed so that the garment may be returned to its original state without telltale creases.

PROTECTING MERCHANDISE FOR SHOWS IN AN OUTSIDE LOCALE

Many shows are given away from the normal home of the clothes that are shown—in television studios, hotel ballrooms, theaters, auditoriums, clubs. Since clothes suffer great wear and tear when they are moved around, special care is demanded to prevent unusual losses and damage. This is one reason many stores have a policy against ever giving fashion shows outside the store.

Containers for Transporting

Special containers are essential for transporting clothes outside of the store. They cannot be sent open on racks because of soilage, damage, and losses.

For a few pieces going to a television studio, a garment bag will suffice because the fashion director usually takes them out and returns them. Care must be taken so that the clothes will not be crumpled en route, since most studios have no facilities for pressing. Best to pack a bit of tissue in bodices and sleeves. The use of garment bags for larger shows is awkward and inefficient. If a few pieces are boxed for a small show, be generous with tissue paper.

Retail stores that produce fashion shows regularly will find it an economy to have special containers made for show purposes. Even though they do not put on shows for outside organizations, they often travel shows to their own branches.

Containers may be any one of several types most generally in use, depending on the frequency of shows outside the store and the usual size of these shows. Some method of locking the containers must be available, such as a padlock. If a combination lock is used, there will never be a problem of arriving at a destination without keys. Valuable furs and jewelry should be under special guard at all times.

The safest containers are wooden or metal "tanks" or wardrobes with a hanging rod inside and rollers on the bottom that may be handled easily by delivery men or truckers. These need to be tall enough for normal clothes to hang, leaving space below for boxes of shoes and accessories. Another good type of container is a pipe rack for hanging with a wooden shelf or canvas sling bottom for accessories. A zipped canvas covering goes over all. Additional accessories may be packed in suitcases or hampers. If carriers are brightly colored, such as in red, yellow, or pink, they are easily identified.

In other cases where merchandise is moved only occasionally and these special carriers are unavailable, wardrobes may be rented in some places (check "Wardrobes" in the yellow pages of the telephone directory or a local mover). Failing this, use pipe racks, covering them completely with canvas or sheets, and tying them all around with cord.

Fixing Responsibility

In sending out a show, merchandise must be checked four times: as it leaves, as it is received at the locale, after the show, and when it arrives back home. A lineup of the show suffices for this.

Responsibility for sending and receiving at both ends should be fixed so that there is no area for a slip.

A dressing room full of beautiful clothes is an invitation to theft. Whenever clothes are left unattended, the room should be double-locked with only one person authorized to have it opened. If it is necessary to store clothes in a hotel overnight or over a weekend, the protection department of the hotel can double-lock the room. However, the person who witnesses the locking must be on hand to have the room opened.

When it is not possible to double-lock a room, it is an economy to have a guard on duty at any time the room is left alone.

Checking in Clothes after a Show

Dressers can be used to advantage in checking and packing after a show. Ask each one to hang, zip, button, belt, and check each outfit as her model returns to the dressing room. The dresser should be able to keep up unless her model has one fast change after another. In this way, the whole show will be back in order within a few minutes after the last number is shown. This is also desirable because helpers in a dressing room tend to disappear very rapidly after a show.

Ask the dressers to make one last check at the end to be sure everything is there, including accessories back in bags or boxes. Any missing pieces should be reported to the person in charge of the show so that an immediate search can be made.

Assistants then place clothes and accessories back on racks or in carriers for return to the fashion director's office. Instructions are given in advance about pickup and delivery back to the store. From there, they go back to the various departments to be checked in and receipted for by the buyer or other authorized person.

10

All about The Models

In the 1930s the movie star was the criterion of feminine glamour. She connoted beauty, fabulous clothes, and wealth. The fashion model has assumed the same aura today. Every girl dreams of being a fashion model, and modeling schools flourish in every city. The most conservative woman's club member secretly sees herself as a chic model on a runway.

Good models are not that easy to come by. However, runway models, with whom we are concerned here, are less difficult to find than photographic models who must have an extra dimension before a camera. So many would-be models believe that a pretty face is the requisite, when actually a not-so-pretty face may be preferred as more chic and more interesting. Balenciaga, who was the dean of Paris couturiers for two decades, was known for his ugly models — but they could show clothes magnificently. An agency named "Ugly" was opened in London in 1969 to supply male and female models who have faces that are interesting rather than handsome or pretty.

Many attributes combine to make an ideal fashion show model:

- She has a flair for fashion and a natural instinct about combining clothes and accessories.
- She fits into the clothes with minimal or no alterations. This means the ideal size and height for the size range she is modeling.
- She has good hair and skin, although hairpieces can solve a hair problem.
- She is objective and willing to wear clothes that she may not like personally.
- She is naturally immaculate and well-groomed.
- She is cooperative with show staff and other models.

- She appreciates the clothes and has empathy with the audience so that the latter will be sold on the former.
- She realizes that modeling is business, and is businesslike about appointments and bookings.

THE AMERICAN MODEL

You have seen in Chapter 2 that modeling is only a little more than a hundred years old, having started around the mid-nineteenth century with the wife of Charles Frederick Worth, the first couturier. Thus modeling started with the live modeling of clothes, rather than with photographic modeling.

At the time of the *Vogue* show in 1914, there was only a handful of professional models who worked for private dressmakers, although fashion photography had begun in 1913 when Baron Gayne de Meyer went to work for *Vogue*. (Edward Steichen is reported to have made fashion photographs in Paris as early as 1911, although his regular work for *Vogue* did not begin until 1923.) For this history-making show, *Vogue* had to advertise for models, although the stars of the show were the society women who lent their names and support to the event.

From then on, the need for professional models gradually grew. They continued to be recruited from those who were working in shops or from society until enterprising John Robert Powers came on the scene.

John Robert Powers and His Agency

Powers was a native of Easton, Pennsylvania, and had been an actor for ten years. Around 1921, finding himself out of work, he answered a photographer's newspaper advertisement for models. Since the photographer needed eight, Powers brought in a group of his out-of-work friends. In his book, *The Powers Girls*, he tells how his wife suggested starting an agency to fill this apparent need.

The new John Robert Powers agency compiled a catalog with pictures of forty friends and sent it to all prospective users of models. This established modeling as a real profession, with the first professional models coming from the theater. Through his effort to "sell" his clients, Powers encouraged the use of models and thus contributed a great deal to the growth of the profession.

The word "model" had come into use before the Powers agency was born, but he preferred the word "subject" which he felt was more professional. Also, his first models were the subjects of photographs.

In gradually changing the type of model he handled, Powers looked

John Robert Powers who opened the first model agency when he saw a need for this service.

for those with whom women could identify, rather than the theatrical type. Of this search, he wrote in his book:

"The secret of effectiveness of models, of course, is in that process of identification by the purchaser and the model. It lies in that dim, unexpected hope, "If I wear that, I will look like that." . . . So that Powers girls emerged, the natural girl, without excessive makeup, without the mincing artificial walk associated in the popular imagination with models. Instead, she is poised, charming, graceful, a model for any woman to follow." [Reprinted from *The Powers Girls* by permission of the author.]

Growth of the Modeling Profession

During the depression of the early 1930s, debutantes and society women modeled professionally to add to shrinking incomes. This probably led to the first modeling school which was operated by Alice and James Dowd, Jr., in New York.

Although other modeling agencies were organized on the Powers pattern, including one by the Dowds named Models Preferred, Powers reigned as the model king for some twenty-five years. Today the big New York model agencies tend to specialize in either photographic or fashion-show models. Eileen Ford, formerly a well-known model, has built up a famous agency of the former type. Gillis MacGil, probably the greatest fashion-show model of all time, heads her own Mannequin Fashion Models Agency for fashion-show models.

The photographic model, whose likeness is seen by millions, has become the peer among models in earnings and prestige. The top ones are recognized as celebrities, and their autographs are sought. Prestige fashion shows such as the big Fashion Group shows of couture and designer clothes, and the Fashion Critics' Awards have added luster to the

Eileen Ford of Ford Model Agency that specializes in photographic models, but handles a few fashion show models.

Gillis MacGil during her successful modeling career as designer Scaasi fits a new design on her.

runway model and have made celebrities of several of them, such as Gillis MacGil.

As a rule, the two types of model do not interchange. Each is a specialist and is not necessarily equipped to handle the other kind of assignment. Many photographic models freeze on a runway, while many runway models freeze before a camera. If she is really famous, a photographic model, such as Jean Shrimpton, may appear as a celebrity in a fashion show.

PROFESSIONALS PREFERRED

With few exceptions, professional models are preferred to amateurs because they have acquired the necessary attributes. They have been trained professionally or have learned through experience how to work efficiently and effectively.

Teen and college clothing looks better on "real" girls. Furthermore, the believability is stronger for this age group when they see fashions modeled by their peers.

Professional models are not only insurance for a good show, but can be a tremendous aid to the fashion director:

- They work impersonally in a businesslike way, understanding the bedlam of the dressing room.
- They are able to handle emergencies and land on their feet.
- Because of their love of clothes and their experience in working with clothes, they are often able to make excellent suggestions about the merchandise and the accessorizing. They are also able to do some of the footwork of assembling accessories.
- They know how to care for clothes and how to prepare them to go back in stock after the show.
- Pros know how to put emphasis on the clothes and "sell" them.

The fashion director and show producer will encounter serious drawbacks when using inexperienced persons as models:

- They may not realize that the fashion show is a business for the store or manufacturer who is providing the clothes.
- They are more personal about the clothes and either resist or refuse to wear anything they dislike personally—or that they think their husbands will dislike!
- Stores are always nervous about offending a customer, especially one who may threaten to close a charge account, and thus feel they must handle amateur models with special care.
- Nonprofessionals do not always keep appointments on time and occasionally do not even appear for the show.
- The inexperienced model works much more slowly than the pro.
- On the runway the difference between amateurs and pros is the difference between amateur theatricals and Broadway.
- Amateurs are harder to fit than professionals because they come in all sizes, heights, and weights.
- They do not know how to care for and handle the merchandise, and damages occur.

The Male Model

Use professional male models if they are available. The fashion show runway is not the place for the average man who feels foolish and uncomfortable modeling in a fashion show. Most men would refuse in the first place.

If there is no model agency to supply professionals, you may be able to book young men who attend an acting or dancing school, a university, or men who belong to a local little theater group. These would at least be at ease before an audience.

When a show is given for a special group, such as a club or a convention, the members may enjoy modeling. Certainly the audience enjoys seeing its own members on the runway. At a show for doctors in a medical group and their wives, one store used professional female models, and doctors as male models. The doctors on and off the runway loved it.

Child Models

While almost anything that children do on a runway is charming and amuses the audience, children who model professionally are preferable when planning a show of young clothes. The agency which handles a child schools the mother in fashion-show conduct for both the child and herself. The children know what to expect:

- They have learned how to work in a businesslike way, even if they are too young to understand the whole thing.
- They understand that strangers are going to dress them and handle them.
- They are not frightened by the stage or runway or by the audience.
- Their mothers understand the business of modeling and realize their responsibilities when accompanying the child to a show: to watch over the child, but not to get in the way or interfere.
- Their parents are aware of child school and labor laws, and can be depended on to secure any necessary papers or permits.

In one big show, an inexperienced tiny tot of about three was pushed before the footlights and an audience of 1000. Her terror was evidenced by her screams. Nothing could budge her until her mother came out and carried her in her arms down the runway. Aside from the harm done to the child, it was an uncomfortable moment for the audience and a strike against the show.

Many stores like to use the children of customers rather than professionals because they consider it good public relations and a drawing card for the show. To obtain names, they ask salespeople in the children's departments to keep an eye out for appealing children, or to keep a registry where mothers may submit candidates. A gift or a gift certificate is sent as a thank-you to skirt any child labor problems. Some fashion directors feel that these mothers are easier to work with than those of professional children because they are less aggressive. They are genuinely interested and cooperative.

Another good source for child models is a ballet or dancing school. These students are likely to feel at home on a stage because they participate in recitals.

When using child models, especially nonprofessionals, rehearse them well at least once so that they know what to expect and are not afraid. Then never change the instructions. Use the same dresser for each child that you will use in the show so that the child will be acquainted with this person.

At the rehearsal, explain carefully to the mothers how the show will be handled backstage and exactly what their responsibilities are. It's a good idea to have a mimeographed schedule to hand out to the mothers with explicit instructions.

THE SOURCES FOR MODELS

When a business or organization plans a fashion show, it usually has in mind who will model the clothes. The fashion show director who handles shows regularly should keep a card file of her sources by type — children, teens, juniors, and so on. A simple three-inch by five-inch or five-inch by eight-inch card is sufficient with the following information:

Female Model

Name _____ Phone ____
Address _____
Agency _____ Phone ____
Height ____ Weight ____ Age or Type __
Hair Color _____ Eyes _____
Dress Size ___ Bust ____ Waist __ Hips __
Gloves ____ Shoes _____ Stockings _____
Comments _____

Male Model

Name _____ Phone ____
Address _____
Agency _____ Phone ____
Height ____ Weight ____ Age or Type _
Hair Color _____ Eyes _____
Neck Size _____ Waist Size _____
Suit Size _____ Shirt Size _____
Shoe Size _____ Sock Size _____
Comments _____

Use white cards for female models, since females are the most frequently booked. Employ yellow cards for male models. This will make filing and using the cards much easier. On the reverse side of the cards may be noted the shows or dates when they have modeled, or any other comments.

As a checklist, the major sources for models are discussed here.

Direct Applicants

Many women and girls who want to model contact possible employers directly, especially stores. This is a good source of adding new types and ages. Establish hours and days for screening applicants in order to save time.

Model Agencies

Because professional models are now so much in demand, agencies to handle this business exist in almost all the large cities. Department stores, manufacturers, and others who regularly employ models, use the services of these agencies who book their models on an hourly, daily, or job basis.

If you are unfamiliar with the leading local agencies, the best way to find out who they are is to ask one of these regular users — the fashion director of a department store, the designer or owner of an apparel manufacturing company. Chances are that the women's page editor of a local newspaper can also supply this information.

Model agencies are listed under the unusual heading of "Models— Living" in the yellow pages of the telephone directory, but it is difficult

In her busy Mannequin Fashion Models Agency in New York, Gillis MacGil takes a booking for a model over the telephone.

to know which of these are the best ones. A telephone call may give you the clue to whether an unknown agency is the type you wish to work with. A personal visit to the agency can certainly provide this information.

Modeling Schools

In almost every city there are modeling schools that appeal for the most part to young women in their teens and twenties. There are also several national chains of modeling schools. Some of these maintain an agency within the school. If not, they at least attempt to help their students and graduates obtain bookings. Inquire locally for the names of reliable schools. These are also listed, along with the agencies, under "Models—Living" in the yellow pages.

Other Schools

Students of ballet, dancing, or drama schools, and of other schools of the performing type may sometimes be engaged for fashion shows. In this case, be very careful in giving instructions, since students are occasionally cavalier about their appointments. Also, when transmitting messages to students through school offices, be sure the message will be given to the student accurately and in time to take action—not just posted on a bulletin board that the student may never see.

Many of the leading professional models refuse to wear lingerie, girdles, and bras in a show, but ballet or dance students may be willing to do this. On the other hand, dancers may have muscles that are too well developed to look well in other fashions on a runway.

Teen Models

Any teen girl will model at the drop of a hat. Many stores have teen fashion boards from which models may be drawn. High schools may refer potential models, but be sure the school understands that size and fashion flair are the criteria for selecting, and not grades.

Society Models

Many shows use members of so-called "society" as the models. This may be a big charity benefit that society women (or men or children) lend their names and time to. It gives the charity well-known names as attractions for drawing an audience. A commercial fashion show may want society models for the prestige value and be willing to make a cash donation to the models' favorite charities as payment.

This is probably the most difficult model to work with. The woman with the biggest name, for example, may also have the biggest figure. It is touchy to ask these women to come for a tryout so that the best sizes and figures may be chosen. Thus it may develop that rather than having models who fit into the clothes and enhance them, it is necessary to find fashions that fit each model and that enhance her. This is not the best way to fit a show.

Women who are active socially can't always come at the most convenient time for fittings and rehearsals, so appointments have to be made to their convenience. Another possible problem is the ego of some of the women which makes them difficult to work with. They don't realize that it is work and expect to be catered to. Also, special comforts, food, and beverages may have to be provided for them.

To obtain society models when they are not known personally, try to find a friend or business associate who has entrée to the social group or who knows one person well enough to make a contact for you. If you are representing a well-known organization, a letter on its writing paper is the best approach. All details should be clearly spelled out. If you can persuade one leader to work with you and become enthusiastic, she can refer you to her friends, or enlist them herself. This is how Edna Woolman Chase was able to succeed with the first fashion show, by interesting Mrs. Stuyvesant Fish in influencing her friends.

Society women are used to wearing good clothes, so it is a mistake to ask or expect them to model really inexpensive clothes. The fashions should be at least middle to upper bracket in price. Couture or designer clothes are very appropriate.

Members of Clubs

When a club or organization plans a show, the committee may suggest that members model. The only benefit that might accrue from this is that members are often tempted to buy the clothes they model. The disadvantages of using nonprofessionals have been discussed and must be weighed against any such benefit. Most fashion directors, when undertaking a show for an organization, stipulate that professional models must be used. If members are used, it is wise either to specify the heights and sizes that can model, or to have a tryout where the best potential models may be selected.

MODEL FEES

Professional models work on an hourly, daily, or job basis. They may handle their own bookings and billings. However, in most cities, agencies handle the best models. The agent makes the bookings, informs the models, bills and collects from the client for the models' work. In turn, he pays the models, deducting his fee, which is usually 10%. Some agencies also bill the client in an equal amount, so that their total fee is 20% of what the model earns.

The client pays for all of the time a model is used—fittings, rehearsals, and show time. On an hourly basis, this can run into a considerable expense. In this case, the terms should be discussed with the agent in an effort to arrive at one lump fee to cover the entire job. Models are customarily not paid for travel time from one job to another unless they actually have to travel from one city to another, and then time and expenses are paid for.

Fees vary widely depending on location and the model herself. For fitting, rehearsal, and show in some places it may be as little as $15–20, while in New York it may soar to as much as $250–300.

Amateur models are recompensed in various ways, or not at all:

- When club members are modeling at a club show, they may model free as a service to the club or as an honor.
- Society models, unless professionals, usually prefer not to be in the position of modeling for a fee. They may request that in lieu of payment to them, a contribution be made to their favorite charity. For a charity benefit, they may donate their services.
- Stores frequently reimburse teen-age nonprofessional models with gift or merchandise certificates to be used in the store.

The important point is that the nonprofessional model understand from the beginning exactly how much time is involved and exactly what the payment will be, if any.

WHEN AND HOW TO BOOK MODELS

Good models are in big demand, especially during peak seasons — when manufacturers are showing their seasonal lines and stores are launching a new season. To obtain the best models and a cross-section of different types, they should be booked as far in advance as possible. This can be three to six months ahead for a major fashion show. Certainly, it should be a month in advance for any kind of show.

The model or agent must be given the exact times and places to appear. Since you are paying for it, the booking should be for a minimum amount of time, yet not be so limited that it will lead to trouble.

The fitting time required will depend on how many outfits the model is to wear. Accessorizing must be done during the fitting so a little extra time is allowed for this. A comfortable amount of time for a model who is to wear three or more outfits is an hour. Two or three models can be fitted at the same time if the fitting staff is well organized.

Although models don't come in dress sizes, they must be able to fit into standard sizes. A slim model wears clothes best, so those who can wear sizes 8, 10, and 12 are preferred for a showing of misses sizes, according to a survey among retail store fashion directors. Size 10 is most important. They must be tall enough to be impressive on a runway — 5 ft. 6 in. to 5 ft. 8½ in., with 5 ft. 8 in. preferable. If the merchandise is in junior sizes, the model must be shorter — 5 ft. 4 in. to 5 ft. 6½ in. — and be able to wear sizes 7 and 9, with the latter more important. In women's clothing, size 14 is ideal, but some 16s and half sizes should be included.

Gillis MacGil's agency, which supplies many models to New York designers, prefers heights of 5 ft. 7 in. to 5 ft. 7½ in. who wear a size 6 or 8, and 5 ft. 7½ in. to 5 ft. 8½ in. who can model sizes 8 or 10. Her shortest model is 5 ft. 6¾ in. who can wear a junior 7 or a misses 6 or 8.

When adult male models are used, size 40 regular is best in a suit or jacket, and a height of at least 5 ft. 10 in. Child models, of course, depend on the children's size range to be shown.

WHAT MODELS ARE EXPECTED TO SUPPLY

Although there may be spares as a regular part of fitting and dressing room supplies, there are certain basics that a professional model knows she is expected to have as her equipment:

- Appropriate undergear in light and dark colors for whatever type apparel she is modeling, such as an evening bra for an evening dress.
- Regular nylon hosiery in a neutral color. Any special hosiery in colors or patterns should be supplied to her along with other accessories.
- A basic wardrobe of shoes in black and neutral colors. Shoes appropriate for each outfit should be provided for her as an accessory but, when shoes are not available, a model must wear her own.
- Her own makeup unless this is being done by a cosmetic company representative or a makeup artist.
- Scarf or other head covering to protect her hairdo, and to keep cosmetics or lipstick from harming the clothes when making a change.
- Dress shields to protect clothing from perspiration.

THE MODELS' MAKEUP AND HAIR

The makeup and hair styling a model wears must be appropriate for the clothing she is modeling. For sportswear and daytime fashions, makeup and hair should be in a style appropriate for when and where the clothes would normally be worn. However, makeup needs to be intensified for a runway or stage because of the strong spotlights—more eye makeup, more coloring on the cheeks, and a brighter lipstick.

Nothing is more ludicrous than an evening hairdo worn with casual clothes. A model must be able to change her hair style when she changes into formal clothes unless she wears a simple style throughout. Today there are excellent wigs and hair pieces that can be pinned on quickly to add glamour. There is usually not time for an elaborate hairdo to be created between changes.

Enlisting Professionals for Credit

To have the best possible look for all models, it is desirable to have both a hair stylist and a makeup artist as a part of the dressing-room staff. In this way, a definite fashion statement can be made about the beauty and hair looks that the fashion director of the show believes in. These beauty professionals can also be sure that each model has a total look before stepping out on the runway.

Since it is costly (but well worth it) to have these specialists, it is often possible to obtain them by giving a prominent credit for makeup and hair styling in the printed program, and also by asking the commentator to call special attention to their work during the show.

In a retail store, the store's own cosmetic department and hairdressing salon may be enlisted to handle this aspect of the show. They should be given the same prominent credit as a favor to them and a service to the audience.

THE MODELS' MANNERS

Models are expected to abide by a code of manners embracing two sets of rules, one for handling the clothes and one for the fitting and dressing rooms. This is based on two needs:

1. The merchandise must be kept in perfect condition so that no damages or losses occur and it may be sold at regular price after the show.
2. The fitting and dressing rooms are work rooms and call for complete cooperation from the models.

Manners to Protect the Merchandise

Professional models are expected to know and observe the following rules, but it is a good idea to post them in the dressing room. The professional model:

1. Wears dress shields to protect clothing from perspiration that could cause the merchandise to have to be marked down or that could make it totally unsalable.
2. Arranges clothes she will model in the most convenient way for

quick changes to avoid damage from fast handling — zippers un-zipped and buttons unbuttoned.

3. If expected to pin price tickets, she does it carefully so that they will not injure merchandise. If tickets are to be removed, the model places them wherever requested so that they may be put back on.

4. She dresses and undresses by putting clothes over the head, but is careful to cover her face with a scarf or other protection to prevent stains on the clothing from makeup or lipstick.

5. After modeling or after the show, she puts all merchandise back on hangers, zips and buttons it. Tickets are unpinned. Accessories are replaced in bags or boxes. Shoes are put back in their boxes, but boxes left open so they may be checked before going back into stock.

6. She never sits down after she is dressed so that clothes will be clean and wrinkle-free.

Manners in the Fitting and Dressing Rooms

The professional model:

1. She makes cooperation her motto.

2. She wears without protest any clothes and accessories the fashion director requests, and only that. She may make suggestions, but bows to the fashion director if she does not agree. The model is there to sell clothes — not to select what she likes.

3. She follows all instructions about how the clothes are to be worn and accessorized. Here, she may also make suggestions, but the fashion director is the last word.

4. She keeps conversation to a minimum before and during a show. When it is necessary to talk, she does so in a low tone so that voices are not heard by the audience.

5. She cooperates with other models in every way, as well as with the show staff.

6. She dresses quickly and lines up promptly for cues.

7. She follows instructions of the producer or choreographer about action on the stage or runway.

8. If photographs are being taken, she tries to give the photographer a chance to snap, but doesn't stop the show to pose.

9. She listens to the commentator and is guided by what she hears while on the runway or stage.

10. She arrives promptly for fittings, and at least half an hour before show time or at the appointed hour — already fed and watered.

11. She observes no smoking and no drinking rules.
12. She does not bring family or friends backstage, and makes only necessary business phone calls.

HOW A MODEL CORRECTLY SHOWS CLOTHES

Throughout fashion-show history, there have been many fashions in how the models walk and show clothes on a runway. Since *Vogue's* first show in 1914, models have come a long way. In describing that event, Emily Post was intrigued by the mannequins' walk (*Vogue*, December 1, 1914):

". . . it might be called the 'manikin dip.' It is a combination of a drop, a twist, and a motion suggesting the famous line, 'She thinks she is swimming.' The dipper takes a step forward, then sinks as though on a spring gone soft, twists herself into a sort of recovery, and manages to propel her body forward another step."

The fashion in modeling today is probably more natural than at any other time. Certainly models don't have to be contortionists as they apparently were in 1914. Now the model stands straight and walks naturally so that the audience may identify easily.

The Entrance

If models are posed on a stage before the curtain opens, each one quickly assumes her place on cue. As each individual model's name is called or her cue given, she moves quickly.

When the model comes on the stage or runway from the wings or from another room, she starts quickly and with a firm step as the starter cues her. She walks with toes pointed straight forward in a natural step. Head is held straight and a smile is always welcome (unless for a very high fashion show where a sophisticated effect is sought). When she reaches the center of the stage or the beginning of the runway, she pauses for a second before starting to walk.

On the Runway

An audience wants to see action, and clothes are best shown with movement. Thus the model keeps moving once she has started down the runway. She pauses to pivot at the points the fashion director has specified.

When she has completed her showing, she leaves the runway quickly, taking care not to stumble on steps. She returns to her station in the dressing room as rapidly as possible. She can often start taking off gloves or unbuttoning a coat or jacket en route to save a precious second or two.

The Pivot

A model turns or pivots on a runway or stage to let the audience have a good look at both front and back of the garment. Beginners or nonprofessionals are self-conscious about the pivot which is very simple to do. At the point of pivot, the model stops in the middle of a step with one foot forward. For some it is easier to have the right foot forward, while for others it is easier with the left foot. She then pivots on the balls of her feet until her body is halfway around, facing in the opposite direction. She takes one step in that direction, stops and completes the turn by pivoting halfway around again in the same direction. The turn is now finished and she walks forward naturally.

Depending on the length of the runway, a pivot looks natural when done halfway down the runway and again at the end before the model goes off.

If a nonprofessional matron finds pivoting difficult, she should be permitted to walk and turn in whatever way is easiest and most natural for her. Teen girls love to learn the pivot because it makes them feel like professional models.

Male models never pivot since it has an unmasculine look. They pause and simply turn around or walk back a few steps before proceeding down the runway. Children walk straight down the runway unless they are old enough to be taught to turn.

Dancing on the Runway

The widespread use of live combos or bands as part of the entertainment at fashion shows has led to dancing on the runway or stage. Because of the loud sound, it has also led to less commentary. It certainly does enliven a show.

A show is also given an extra fillip when models can execute a little routine at certain appropriate points in the show. One show made excellent use of this idea to point up especially snappy or dramatic merchandise. For example, a white bunny fur skirt with slinky mat jersey shirt was repeated on a dozen models who did a simple routine against a background of bunny rabbits projected on multiscreens.

The problem here is finding models who can show clothes off to best advantage, and at the same time dance or perform well enough to appear before an audience. The Milliken Breakfast Show has always used professional dancers from the theater, but their bodies and stances are not those of the good model. Their legs are muscular and not the model's ideal legs. In this case, the theatricality, humor, and excitement of the entire show overshadow these drawbacks. Good models would show the clothes to better advantage, but they would be unable to perform the dances and songs.

The decision must be made as to which is more important—that the clothes look their best, or that the performers are the best. In most fashion shows, it is the former.

A good choreographer can do a great deal toward giving the models a professional look on the runway and can teach them simple routines. Most attractive young models today are also good dancers of popular steps. It takes just a little sound to get them started.

Don't Point

Using the forefinger or hand to point to details on an outfit or to the accessories as the commentator mentions them is nonprofessional. It can be assumed that the audience knows where to look for the "white linen collar" or the "small satchel handbag." The models should be instructed to keep walking naturally while such details are being described.

Handling Accessories and Props

Models must remember not to hold a handbag or an umbrella in front of the garment. A bag should be carried as one would normally carry it. An umbrella may be tucked under the arm, carried like a cane, or even opened if it does not obstruct the view.

In tune with more streamlined shows, hand props are not carried as much as they have been in the past, but they are sometimes appropriate. The only caution here is the same as that for accessories. Props should never be held in a way that they hide details of the outfit. They should never be so large that they are difficult or awkward for the model to handle. An example is luggage which is sometimes included in a fashion show. A model can easily carry a small tote, but should not be expected to struggle down a runway with a big suitcase.

Removing Jackets and Coats

When a model is showing more than one piece, such as a dress with a jacket or a coat over a dress, the audience will at least want a peek at the garment underneath.

After the model has shown the entire outfit sufficiently for the entire audience to see the total look, she quickly unbuttons the jacket or coat while continuing to walk. If the buttons are difficult to handle or numerous, it may be wise to carry the gloves, if any, so that she can cope better. She then slips out of the jacket or coat as quickly as possible, folds it over one arm, and continues to walk and pivot until everyone has been able to see the dress.

If it is too difficult or it would take too much time to take the outer garment off entirely, it can be dropped back off the shoulders sufficiently for the inside garment to be seen. As the model leaves the runway, she can shrug it back onto her shoulders.

Following the Commentator

Models must be trained to listen to the commentator, if any. She (or he) may have little to say about some outfits and a great deal about others. The rehearsal indicates to the model how long she is expected to be on the runway, but sometimes the commentator adds an impromptu thought which throws the timing off. The model remains on the runway and keeps moving until the commentator has finished talking about her.

Modeling Special Clothes

Since very few human beings are perfect in appearance from top to toe, there are excellent models who are not perfect beauties. Some have marvelous bodies, but plain faces. Some have great beauty, but bad legs. Some few haven't a great deal to offer in physical appearance, but have such spirit, life, and rapport on the runway that they become good models.

The physical makeup of the model must be considered in relation to the type of clothes she is to wear. Coats and suits, which are of a heavier construction, can cover up many body defects but may tend to swallow up a fragile girl. For clothes that show off the body, such as snug sweaters or soft dresses, the body must be good. Evening clothes should be worn by girls with pretty faces, arms, and bosoms. A short evening dress calls for good legs too.

Swimsuits demand a model with an excellent figure and good legs. A too-thin swimsuit model with skinny arms and legs looks emaciated and pitiful on the runway. An overly developed girl is not attractive in a swimsuit. At the beginning of the season, white models may appear too pale to be attractive. A tiny bit of leg makeup will provide a healthier look. Black models look especially well in swimsuits if the colors of the suits are carefully chosen.

Finding models for girdles, bras, and lingerie is difficult. The old criterion for a foundation model was a well-developed body. However, that has changed, and a model with a good overall figure and legs, as for swimsuits, is preferable. A pretty, refined face is helpful to give a refined overall look.

INFORMAL MODELING

Informal modeling does not have the stringent requirements of runway modeling, but it does have some special prerequisites. The most important of these is warmth and friendliness toward the audience. Although a model on a runway must have a rapport with the audience to be successful, the informal model has a direct personal contact with those for whom she is modeling. A sincere smile is her best tool in winning them over.

In choosing informal models, be sure they are resourceful and responsible since they are out there on their own. They must be counted on to do their work quickly and well, to change without aid, and to return to the audience.

Tearoom or Restaurant Modeling

The model who works in a tearoom or restaurant in a store, hotel, or club must be able to arrange her outfits and accessories for easy changes without a dresser to help. She does not have to change as quickly as the girl in a fashion show and can take five minutes or so.

When dressed, she walks naturally among the tables, covering the entire room. Depending on the number of tables, she should pause and pivot at each. She may even speak to the occupants of the table, giving the department location where the merchandise may be found in the store, or the name of the store if modeling in a hotel or club. Someone will always ask the price too. She must be clever enough to move from table to table without becoming involved in a conversation.

Departmental or Storewide Modeling

Some fine stores retain models to walk through the store or model within one department. In this situation, the audience consists of customers who are rushing through. They may glance at the model, but the general public is shy about approaching a stranger with questions.

A model in this situation has to be sensitive as to when a customer is interested. She then takes the initiative by offering information: "This hostess gown is from our Chez Vous Boutique on the fifth floor. They have it in coral too. Wouldn't you like to go up and try it on." There is no need to mention price in informal modeling unless asked.

When a model is assigned to one department only, she can approach customers as she would in a restaurant.

Modeling for Store Personnel

As part of their sales training, some stores wisely have models put on new fashions and circulate through fashion departments before the store opens in the morning. It may be merchandise that is advertised that day or in the windows. The model should try to see as many of the pertinent personnel as possible. It is essential that she tell them exactly why she is showing the clothes (new in store, advertised, in window), and where they may be found in the store. Any new fashion points should be made: "This is the new St. Laurent pants look we advertised in the *Dispatch* this morning. It's in the Country Club shop on the third floor—$90 for both pieces together."

TELEVISION MODELING

Modeling before the TV camera is one of the most difficult assignments, even for a professional model. The good runway model may not be photogenic. The star photographic model is used to a frozen stance and may not be able to move. An actress may not look well in the clothes and may tend to demonstrate her thespian talent rather than sell the clothes. Fashion on TV has not advanced to the point where there are specialists in this kind of modeling.

For the vast heterogeneous audience, look for an all-American type (unless it is for an ethnic station)—attractive, warm, at ease. The chic high-fashion model is not appropriate because she is alien to the environment of the majority of the audience. The exception is for an import or couture show where a sophisticated feeling is to be projected.

These several additional tips will help you obtain the best effect when modeling fashion on television:

- Select models who can move easily. Although movement is limited by camera range, the model will be more at ease if she is given something to do. Plan some special action for her if possible.
- Remember that the camera adds about ten pounds to anyone's appearance, so models should be thinner than the usual runway model.
- Have enough models so that each one is not kept on camera too long. Because movement is limited, a model tends to take on a

frozen look or become embarrassed if the camera is focused on her too long.

- In many places there are strict union requirements for television models. The station will probably volunteer this information, but be sure to have an explicit understanding about what the models are to do before the camera (this controls the fees) and what the fees will be.

SHOWROOM MODELING

Manufacturers and designers show their collections or designs at certain market times. This takes place in the salon or showroom unless a special "opening" is held elsewhere. This type of modeling has special requirements:

- Most collections or showroom samples are made on the girls who will model them. Thus the model must be willing to stand endlessly in the design room, and must have a rapport with the designer. (Many designers even welcome the suggestions of their models, and many models have become designers.)
- The model must be highly dependable because the clothes she will show are made for her.
- She must be able to work quickly and independently in changing without help.
- She must have a friendly, helpful attitude that will put a buyer in a buying mood.
- She must know all about the clothes she shows in order to be able to answer questions and give buyers information about them.
- She must sincerely care about selling the clothes she models because a model can make or break what she wears.
- As for size, shape, and look—that depends on what appeals to the designer and the type of merchandise he creates. Most designers have a special type of wearer in mind.

Showroom modeling is, for the most part, straight showing of the clothes in an established order, one model coming out at a time. The object is to impress the buyers with the merchandise and to have good visibility. Thus the models must be sure that every part of the room is adequately covered and that sufficient pivots are made for everyone to see the complete garment.

Since showroom modeling is specifically for selling, it should not be dressed up with too much entertainment. An exciting or amusing gimmick is always welcome, but a buyer's time should not be taken up this way. Some of the designers of younger fashions have used surprise openings of the showing and live or taped sound to add interest. This is excellent as long as it is a background for showing and selling.

11

Commentator and Commentary

The very first fashion show, *Vogue's* Fashion Fête in 1914, established the precedent for commentators and commentary. Two prominent singers acted as co-commentators and set the scene with their opening patter in playlet form. The female member of the team announced the individual numbers as they came out.

Other early fashion presentations followed the show format with a book and music. Actors, actresses, singers, and dancers were used to unfold the fashion story.

As fashion shows became more common, the commentator became more prominent and often was the star of the show. Retail department and specialty stores began to participate during the 1920's when the new position of "stylist" was created. The famous Tobé (Mrs. Tobé Coller Davis, who died in 1962 at about seventy years of age) originated the job that evolved into today's fashion director or fashion coordinator.

About 1920 Tobé went to work for Franklin Simon, Fifth Avenue's great fashion merchant of the day. She soon began frequenting smart spots and traveling to Paris to report back what the "beautiful people" of that era were doing and wearing. The store wanted to keep *au courant* with their style of living, so the title "stylist" was coined for Tobé.

As other store stylists emerged, they began to arrange fashion shows to promote their stores and show the fashions they offered. In these presentations emphasis was put on the clothes rather than on showmanship, and so the stylist turned commentator to explain the fashion news that was exemplified by the clothes. Models usually came out one by one, with a bride closing the show as the height of beauty and romance. The commentator described each garment in detail, often with gushing superlatives.

The French couture houses have always confined their commentary to calling out each number as the model appears. The signal for the

193

Tobe Coller Davis, known professionally as Tobe, who originated the fashion position of stylist, and was one of the first fashion show commentators.

showing to begin is the appearance of the *directrice* or a *vendeuse* and the first model. The directrice calls the number in French, and possibly also the name of the garment. If there are several salons, there may be an announcer in each room. The signal for the end of the show is the appearance of the bride.

The usual fashion shows — staged productions and straight fashion parades — went along without much change from the standpoint of commentary until the 1960s. It was the prevalence of the new rock sound groups that actually forced a change. Mary Quant's historical press show of 1958 was the precursor of the new show without any commentary that was on the way in.

The teen-age fashion shows given by *Seventeen* in New York and by retail stores across the country during the early 1960s recognized that the rock sound was appreciated by all young people. So this ingredient was added to the fashion show as a major feature, always certain to draw a big young crowd. (It was at this point that young men began to turn up in the audiences.) Against this competition of sound, the commentator was forced to surrender and leave the scene. The sound emerged, the models began to move and to dance, and commentary disappeared. Any explanation that had to be given was made between scenes or groupings, or flashed on a screen.

Producers of shows for adult audiences were captivated by the idea, and commentary became less important in these presentations too. It was suddenly apparent to everyone that a good show projects its own message without the echo of a human voice.

This trend to no commentary has influenced the kind of commentary when it is a part of a show. It is shorter, more to the point, and with fewer adjectives and superlatives. It is used to emphasize fashion information and to instruct.

WHO SHOULD COMMENTATE

Since the purpose of fashion-show commentary is to give information to the audience about the clothes, as a rule the commentator should be someone who knows fashion and knows why the clothes in the show are there.

In a department or specialty store, the person most qualified is the fashion director or coordinator. If it is a teen show put together by a youth coordinator, she is equipped to handle the commentary. This applies to all shows given in or by a store, whether for customers, training, press, or a benefit. Since fashion shows are so much a part of a fashion coordinator's job, most coordinators are quite accomplished at handling this assignment and usually present an attractive fashion-right appearance.

If a trunk show is given in a store, the visitor accompanying the collection certainly knows the clothes, but may be too close to them to give a good objective commentary, and may not have a good stage voice and presence. The fashion coordinator of the store must be aware of whether or not the manufacturer's representative can do a good job. If not, she should handle it, with the visitor either coming in on a co-commentary or simply being introduced and asked to utter a few well-chosen words.

An audience is definitely interested in seeing the visiting authority, who may be the designer. They can then identify this person in the appropriate ready-to-wear department and will feel less hesitant to approach the person for help.

If a store is tying in with a magazine fashion promotion, an editor from the magazine may sometimes be obtained as guest commentator. She naturally knows the fashion story and the clothes. However, she should arrive early enough to attend a rehearsal and go through the lineup of clothes and accessories.

For the showing of a manufacturer's line or a couturier's collection in a showroom or salon, the manufacturer or publicity director is qualified to commentate. Whether a designer should perform this function depends on whether the designer heads the house and whether the designer is an outgoing personality who can speak and sell.

The fashion editor of a magazine or newspaper is the person qualified to handle commentary for a show given by these media.

Shows staged primarily for entertainment, such as a television show, a big benefit, or a theatrical production, demand an extra dimension. The commentator must be as photogenic as possible for TV (the camera

Celebrity commentator Maggi McNellis at the "Fashions on Ice" show, sponsored by The Singer Company to publicize the United Hospital Fund in New York, is muffled in furs, while the model skates in a filmy bridal dress.

Co-commentators for Titche's fashion show in American Airlines' hanger in Dallas perch on a platform above the audience.

adds ten poinds to weight!), and have a stage presence for this and for the other occasions mentioned. Although every commentator has to have empathy with the audience to be successful, anyone who participates in an entertainment show must have this quality in full measure plus a dash of theatricality or "ham." She (or he) must be able to hold and dominate the audience.

Co-Commentators

Having more than one commentator is sometimes desirable. It adds a change of pace and a change of voice to the interest of the show. Female and male voices serve as effective foils for each other. A fashion coordinator of a store and a visiting celebrity — such as a designer, editor, or disc jockey — can heighten the drama of the show.

For a benefit or other entertainment show, there can be one anchor commentator who is a fashion authority plus a succession of co-commentators, a new one for each scene or sequence. This provides an opportunity to show off as many celebrities as can be corralled, which does attract an audience.

Celebrity Commentators

Using celebrities to commentate for a serious fashion show is loaded with danger. Actors and actresses are naturally primarily interested in promoting themselves rather than the clothes, which they probably don't understand. Unless the celebrity is known as someone who does an interesting commentary, or unless a complete script is prepared and followed, it is better to use the celebrity in another way.

If the entertainment value of the celebrity is more important to the show than the fashions that are being shown, let the celebrity emerge as a celebrity and don't worry about the commentary. For example, personalities such as Orson Bean or the Smothers Brothers could undoubtedly entertain an audience with ease and humor, but their commentary would be designed to bring laughs rather than give information. This would be perfect for a big evening benefit attended by both men and women. Someone like Arlene Francis could fill every qualification because she is fashion-knowledgeable as well as being a glamorous celebrity. Good judgment must be used.

When using a celebrity, it's always a good idea to have a substitute in mind. Their time is never their own, so they may have to cancel at the last minute because of a booking or other professional engagement.

HOW THE COMMENTATOR SHOULD LOOK

It goes without saying that anyone who commentates a fashion show should look as if she or he knows what fashion is all about. Apparel must be fashion-right, but not extreme or overdone. Accessories should be carefully chosen but understated in order not to distract the audience. Also, noisy accessories like jangling bracelets or belts are distracting.

If the audience is so expert that it would know the vintage of the commentator's outfit, it should certainly be of the current season. A commentator can easily wear something brand new to introduce the fashion or to promote it. An example is the big fashion for pants that broke out in 1968. Alert commentators immediately adopted these in order to make a fashion point before their audiences.

The commentator's hair must be freshly done and in a style that is appropriate to the time of day. In other words, no fancy evening hair styles for a daytime show. Makeup should also be carefully selected and applied.

A male commentator may wear something with snap, but also should be careful not to outdo the models in the show—unless he is a celebrity.

If it is a retail store show, commentators frequently select something new from stock to wear.

THE COMMENTATOR'S DELIVERY

A good speaking voice is a requisite for anyone addressing an audience unless it is a person whose signature is an unusual voice. Selma Diamond of television fame is an example with her gravelly speech.

A good fashion show commentator speaks clearly and with authority. Her inflection is warm and friendly so that the audience will respond favorably toward her. She never talks down to the audience, nor takes a condescending tone.

A microphone hooked up to a public address system should always be available. It is important for the commentator and electrician to check it out beforehand to be sure it works, is properly adjusted for sound and her voice, and is the right height if it is a standing mike. Also, the commentator should know how to turn it on and off.

Choose any type of microphone except a hand-held one. It is too difficult to juggle notes and a mike at the same time. The commentator needs to have her hands free.

It is essential that the commentator be located where she can see the entry of the models and the stage. If slide or film projection is used, she must be able to see the screen. Otherwise, she is working under the handicap of not being able to see what she is talking about, and could easily lose control of the show.

A podium or lectern for cards, notes, or script makes the commentator's job easier. A glass of water nearby prevents coughing or a dry throat. One well-known commentator experienced a dry throat before a large audience and was forced to stand speechless for several minutes until scurrying aids could find a glass of water.

THE COMMENTARY

Fashion show commentary may take one of three forms:

1. Ad-libbed commentary, based on a thorough knowledge of fashion and the particular clothes in the show.
2. Commentary completely written out and read by the commentator.
3. A complete script of a staged show, including all commentary on the clothes.

The first two methods are used for a straight fashion show, while a script becomes necessary if there is special staging.

If the commentator is experienced and is able to ad-lib, as most fashion directors are, this is preferable to a written commentary. She is better able to pace what she has to say to the model's movements. The audience responds well to ad-libbed commentary because the commentator is talking directly to them which is more convincing and more interesting.

When commenting extemporaneously, the person must be on guard against using the same descriptive words over and over again.

When using a written commentary, the speaker may encounter difficulty in synchronizing what she has to read with the model's pace. She may find that she has more to say, but that the model has left the runway. She may also find it difficult to fill in gaps when a model is late in appearing. These are points to be aware of and to be able to handle with ease. A thorough rehearsal is the best insurance, aside from experience.

Opening the Show

A staged fashion show has a complete script that must be followed with no ad-libbed opening remarks.

If commentary is ad libbed or read from cards, plunge immediately into the show after a pleasant "Good morning" or "Good afternoon" greeting. Quash the nervous inclination to tell the audience you are happy that they got up so early to come to a morning show . . . or that they were wonderful to come out in the rain . . . or other remarks of this type.

Absolutely taboo is going into an explanation that you have a wonderful show planned for them and that they're going to love it. They expect this without your telling them, or they wouldn't have come. There's the further possibility that they may not agree that it was so wonderful after they see it. Let them be the judge.

The Fashion Message

Good commentary tells and sells while the model shows and sells. Make it as bright, crisp, and informative as possible. Cut it short. Catchy phrases, allusions to current events, humor, even clichés make for interesting listening.

The audience is there to learn about new fashion, as well as to be entertained. Thus commentary is best when it points out the fashion news, when it explains how to wear and accessorize fashions, when it evaluates for the viewer.

Totally unnecessary is the enumeration of the color (unless it is a special fashion point) and every detail that the audience can easily see and doesn't need to be told about. Equally taboo is the use of gushy adjectives that contribute nothing to the information given.

WRONG. The next model is wearing a black and white checked suit with notched collar. Black buttons march down the front of the jacket. The long sleeves are adorned with buttoned tabs. The skirt has whirling box pleats. Under the jacket is a striped shirt with a polka dot tie. Her accessories are a yellow handbag, and black patent shoes. (All of this is boring and obvious to the eye. No news is pointed out. The outfit isn't "sold" by the commentator.)

WRONG. Sally, our next glamorous model, looks absolutely ravishing in this marvelous black and white checked suit. The jacket is a dream as it skims over her sylphlike figure, while the pleated skirt flatters her long-stemmed American Beauty legs. And aren't the accessories adorable! (No information of value is given. The descriptive words used mean nothing. The commentator is editorializing with her own opinions, rather than letting the audience decide for themselves whether it is all "ravishing" and "adorable.")

RIGHT. This spring you can express individuality by mixing all kinds of patterns as long as they have one connecting link. In this outfit it's the black and white combo that coordinates the stripe of the shirt and the dot of the tie with the check of the suit. Our model chooses this season's favorite accent to swing along in her taxi yellow satchel with new shoulder chains. (The information given is all news: mixing patterns and how to do it, the season's accent color, and the new shoulder chains of the handbag. Other details are obvious and not important enough to mention.)

To Price or Not

Whether to give the prices of the merchandise being modeled depends on the purpose of the show. If it is a selling show, such as presenting a manufacturer's line or a trade show, where price is essential information, prices may be given by the commentator as a service. However, if there is a program listing prices, there is no need to repeat them in the commentary.

Enumerating the price of every piece or outfit is boring at a consumer show (and anyone who buys from the show doesn't want her friends to know the prices). An occasional price for something special is acceptable and gives variety to the commentary—but only if it is significant, such as a good value or a very high price as a shocker. Otherwise, list prices on the program or leave it to the audience to shop for whatever interests them.

Whether to Credit Manufacturers and Designers

The same kind of judgment involved in giving prices applies to whether to give the manufacturer's or designer's name in a commentary. If it is a designer show, naturally the names of the designers are included as essential information.

To avoid confusion, manufacturers or designers should be credited when a group or several are participating together in one trade show. Even though there is a program, the audience may become confused as to where the merchandise of one leaves off and another begins.

To call out the names of manufacturers who are not known to the general public (the majority are not) contributes nothing to a show. Quite the contrary, it detracts from the excitement and slows the action.

How to Handle the Entry and Exit of Models

It should not be the commentator's responsibility to call the models onto the stage or runway. This is the duty of the starter at the stage entrance. She pushes each model or group out at the proper moment, carefully following a lineup or script held in her hand. However, if the starter fails to have a model out on cue, it is up to the commentator to keep the show flowing. She need not feel that she must provide nonstop patter (an occasional pause is refreshing), but on the other hand she can't afford to lose her audience through a long gap. It is unprofessional and boring to make such comments as, "I guess the next models aren't ready yet — they do have some fast changes," or to call out desperately, "Are the next models ready?"

The solution to filling pauses is to give credits, information about where the merchandise may be purchased, kudos to the music, and anything else of pertinence. Reminders may be jotted down on a card kept separately on the lectern where it may be picked up easily. If the commentator has no lectern, the notes may be made on a colored card so she can quickly pick it out from her deck of commentary cards as needed. Here are some suggested subjects to use as fillers:

- The hair styles and the hairdresser
- The makeup and the makeup artist
- The music group
- Floors and departments where clothes and accessories are located (if a store show)
- The models if they are nonprofessionals, such as the members of a club

• General fashion comments that are pertinent to the show

If a group of models are onstage together, it is wise for the commentator to call the name of each when she is ready for her to start. Otherwise, the models forget their order and either the wrong one starts or no one does.

As for dismissing the models from the runway, a good rehearsal will clue each girl as to how long to remain on the runway so that no directions need be given. However, nonprofessional models are frequently puzzled about when to exit and may simply flee too fast before the commentator has had time to say anything. In this case, the models may be instructed beforehand to keep moving on the runway until the commentator says, "Thank you."

Models tend not to listen to the commentator, so a word of caution before the show is in order. The commentator may want to ask the model to turn around, or to take off a jacket, or to reveal a special lining. If the model listens, she will have no problems about smoothly entering, modeling, and exiting.

There is a question about whether to call the models by name. This is perfectly acceptable and does compliment the model by making her a personality or a star. It is a particularly appropriate gesture when nonprofessionals are used, such as teen-age girls or club members. Teenagers also like to have their schools mentioned along with any special honors such as being a football queen or the like.

What to Do when the Wrong Model Comes out

A wise commentator makes a last-minute check in the dressing room before starting the show, to be sure all the models are there and no changes have been made in the lineup. This eliminates surprises that can upset even the best commentator.

Even though this check is made, errors do happen because the starter is not alert or because a model has an accident. Thus the commentator must keep one eye on who is coming onstage and be ready to shift if necessary. This means that she must always be able to see the stage.

A mixed-up lineup is one of the most difficult situations for any commentator to handle, especially an inexperienced one. To be in a position to smooth over the situation, the commentator needs to know the clothes so well that she is able to pick up and talk about what she sees even if it is a shock. This is one advantage to ad-libbing. If the commentator depends on a written commentary, it is more difficult to find the correct place in her script or to reshuffle her cards. Of course, the no-commentary technique skirts this problem.

The Well-Kept Mishap

The audience is not concerned with mishaps, accidents, or problems that occur during a fashion show. In fact, it embarrasses them. Let any such happening remain a well-kept secret. No comment is the best policy.

On many occasions models have stumbled or have even fallen down the steps of a runway. The audience tends to gasp. The commentator will end with a better show if she takes no note of the accident, but just keeps on going.

Commentary about Door Prizes

Although door prizes have a reason for being in some fashion shows, stopping the show to award prizes detracts from the excitement of the show itself. Holding the drawing after the finale is a real anticlimax and may send the majority of the guests away with a letdown feeling rather than one of excitement. It is preferable to find a spot midway in the show to take care of this chore. Better to stop the show in the middle than to kill it at the end. If there is a break for entertainment, give the prizes before the entertainment in order not to take away from the artists' impact.

Try to make the door prize ceremony fun and exciting by describing the gifts and by calling the numbers with suspense. In most cases, door prizes have been donated by a company that deserves a few complimentary words about the product.

Closing the Show

A staged show naturally has a staged ending—and it ends. A more informal commentary can end with a reminder of where the clothes may be seen and purchased, and with a warm thank-you to the audience. Make it short.

HOW TO PREPARE WRITTEN COMMENTARY

A good written commentary (or script) demands a good writer. Find the best one available. Many talented talkers are at a loss when it comes to putting words on paper. A written show naturally assumes more formality than one that is ad libbed. Thus a professional job is demanded in the writing.

Cards versus a List

Without any question, it is more efficient to write the commentary on cards rather than in a running list. Any changes may be easily and quickly made in a set of cards by switching the cards around, deleting any "drops" or adding new pieces. A running list does not allow for these changes without retyping, or the commentator may find herself with such messy copy that she can scarcely decipher it.

Even though the commentator ad-libs her commentary, she needs numbered cards with the models' names and some identification of the merchandise. It is a good idea to jot down a reminder of any fashion points to be emphasized or any good descriptive words she wants to remember to use in connection with any piece of merchandise.

A 5 in. by 8 in. card provides adequate space for double- or triple-spaced typing for ease of reading. This size also allows room for adding notes. Typing may be in uppercase and lowercase, or all caps, depending on the reader's preference. Some commentators print or write by hand in giant size in order to be able to read without wearing glasses.

A well-written commentary card looks like this:

---

7.   **GENNY BLISS**   **CENTRAL HIGH SCHOOL**
(Number in   (Model's name)   (Model's school)
lineup)

Genny Bliss shows how you can express individuality by mixing all kinds of patterns as long as they have one connecting link. In this outfit, it's the black and white combo that coordinates the stripe of the shirt and the dot of the tie with the check of the suit. Genny chooses this season's favorite accent to swing along in her taxi yellow satchel with new shoulder chain.

End Scene — Music Break Here

For an ad-libbed commentary, this card would look like this:

---

7.   **GENNY BLISS**   **CENTRAL HIGH SCHOOL**
Mixed Patterns — Black/White Checked Suit —
Striped Shirt — Dot Tie
Taxi Yellow Shoulder Chain Satchel.
End Scene — Music Break Here

Flag the beginnings and ends of sequences, music breaks, door prizes, or any other special action in the show with prominent notes. For example, the above card marks the end of a scene with a special music number to follow, as noted at the lower right corner, underscored.

Follow this with an insert card carrying the music information:

SPECIAL SET TO BE PLAYED BY:
THE UPTIGHTS
LANCE KELLY, LEAD VOCALIST

Insert a transition card between each sequence with introductory fashion notes about the upcoming scene:

SCENE III
Strike up the band for fashion's newest note—bandings of contrasting color. Around necklines, circling armholes, streaking down plackets, marking off hems. Favorite note is navy blue banding white.

Commentator Keeps Control of Cards

An unattractive procedure that is sometimes followed is to have each model, as she enters the stage, walk over to the commentator and hand her the card that describes the clothes she is wearing. The theory is that the commentator will then never have the wrong card for the model on the runway (the models sometimes forget to bring the card!).

It is preferable to take a chance on the models' appearing in the right order than to use this awkward device which looks as if the show were put together at the last moment and the commentator had never before seen the clothes. It is also boring for each model to go through the routine of walking to the podium with a card in her hand.

HOW TO PREPARE A COMPLETE SCRIPT

A script for a staged show will be used and followed by everyone participating: commentator, dressing room staff, musicians, entertainers, electricians, stage manager, and director. Therefore, every bit of information must be contained in the script, including action, cues, and commentary.

After the script has been drafted by a good writer, call a meeting of the staff to read it together. Make any necessary changes before reproducing it in quantity. It is a good idea and insurance for a good show to hold a second reading to be sure everyone agrees on the final script. At the same time, individual staff members may make their own notations.

A sample section of a well-prepared fashion-show script follows. Observe how plenty of space is left in margins and throughout the script for additional notes and cues that each participant needs to make. This is no place to save paper. Since slides are used in this imaginary show, the projectionist has to mark his script accordingly. The music director and the lighting director add their notes. Nothing can be left to chance.

"FASHION TAKES A TRIP"
REGENT HOUSE BALLROOM
June 9, 1970

Show Script

PRE-SET STAGE	9 ft by 12 ft movie screen edged in three rows of lights. White platform in front of screen with three steps leading to stage floor. Black back curtain.
PRE-SET BACK-STAGE	Jane Simmons and Ron Phelps, commentators One tour guide Six models for opening scene
INTRODUCTION	Fanfare Houselights down Spot on center curtain Enter Jane and Ronald from center curtain Jane goes to mike right with follow spot Ron goes to mike left with follow spot

Show Begins

AS CURTAIN OPENS, TAPED
SOUND OF BLAST OF ROCK-
ET, WHIRR OF JET, MOTOR
OF CAR. SLIDES OF ROCK-
ETS, JET PLANES, CARS
FLASH ON SCREEN.

JANE: Zzzzzt by rocket . . . zoom by jet . . . or just
                             hum along by car. However and whenever you
                             choose to go, travel in style.
RON: Our tour guide will show you how. Here he
                             comes now to conduct your
CUE: fashion sightseeing tour.

SLIDE   OF   CITY   STREET
COMES ON. GUIDE ENTERS
POINTING UPWARD WITH A
CANE, FOLLOWED BY MOD-
ELS   STARING   UP.   WHEN
ALL   ARE   ON   STAGE,   THEY
"FREEZE" IN THEIR POSES.
THEY PEEL OFF AND MODEL
ON RUNWAY AS COMMEN-
TATORS DESCRIBE EACH.

JANE: Nothing travels like a knit . . . (continues
                             commentary on first model)
RON: But nothing packs like silk jersey . . .
                             (continues commentary on next model)
                             (Alternating commentary continues for the six
                             models.)
GUIDE GOES DOWN
RUNWAY WITH LAST MODEL.
                      (Continue the script in this form.)

PARTIAL COMMENTARY

Commentary on each individual outfit may be eliminated, yet an explanation of new fashion ideas retained if it is felt that an explanation is
needed.

The best way to handle this is to lower the music at the beginning of
each sequence or scene while the commentator makes a short statement
(one or two sentences) about the next fashion grouping:

Fashion slinks, slithers, and shines when the sun goes down. This winter,
you'll find the chic guests at every party wearing body-skimming crepe-
back satins in smoldering colors.

As this brief description of the next group of models ends, let the
music come up and the models come on.

These explanations may be taped by someone with a good voice, if desired, so that only models and performers are on stage throughout the show. This results in a more professional presentation.

Another way in which short bits of information may be given to the audience between sequences is through the use of slides carrying the message. These may be interesting in themselves through the use of varied lettering and colored or textured backgrounds.

12

The Extras that Make a Good Show Great

Knowing the extra ins and outs of producing a successful show will help you plan every detail for maximal success and minimal disappointments.

TICKETS DO TELL

Anyone who produces a show, fashion or otherwise, immediately has a problem of the audience. Everyone wants a full house, but no one wants an irate overflow. Effective publicity will accomplish the first. Tickets will prevent the latter.

If tickets are sold, the only task is to sell them all. Simply stop selling when the supply is exhausted. If a person pays for a ticket, chances are he will come. If cancellations and refunds are permitted, a cutoff date several days before the show will permit cancelled tickets to be resold.

When tickets are distributed free, it is essential to estimate as accurately as possible the number to be given out. People tend to take free tickets whether or not they are sure they can come, and they tend to take more than they need in case a friend wants to come along. Thus a percentage of tickets over and above the number of seats must be distributed to make up for those who have tickets but are "no shows." Approximately one third more tickets than seats should assure a full house. For example, if the house accommodates 900, prepare around 1200 tickets — and make every effort to have them all picked up. Don't distribute a limitless number or you will have a riot on your hands.

When stores distribute free tickets, they usually like to have customers pick them up in the department that is sponsoring the show or providing the majority of the fashions. This brings a stream of persons into the store and into the department. They will usually buy something on

This is your ticket

to the

1969 MILLIKEN BREAKFAST SHOW

THE WALDORF-ASTORIA HOTEL
50th Street and Park Avenue
New York City

TICKET OF ADMISSION TO
1969 MILLIKEN BREAKFAST SHOW

Date: May 27, 1969
Time: Breakfast   7:10-7:50 A.M.
             Show Time 7:55 A.M.
    (No Breakfast Served During Show)
Place: The Waldorf-Astoria
             Grand Ballroom
             50th Street and Park Avenue
             New York City

Keep "Milliken" Badge in this envelope.
Both are necessary for admission.

After May 19 The
Milliken Breakfast Show Committee
can be reached by calling
695-4210, 11, 12, 13, 14

Milliken

welcomes

KAY CORINTH

Ticket to the Milliken Breakfast Show is an identification sticker for each guest to wear, slipped into an envelope with all information about the show.

the way, or at least will know where the department is when they do need the merchandise. For example, tickets for a teen show may be distributed in a junior department or those for a bridal show in the bridal department.

Of course, demand for and use of tickets depends on the type of show. Girls who evidence interest in a bridal show by picking up tickets are usually engaged and have plans for marriage. They are likely to attend. For this reason, it may be necessary to distribute only 10% to 15% additional tickets to assure a full house.

Business girls are more prone to take tickets and not attend. They don't have the immediate motivation that the bride does. In addition, they may be detained by work or simply be too tired to go when the time comes. So half again as many tickets is not a dangerous number to distribute. Some stores have found that serving a light dinner at a nominal charge preceding the fashion show assures a good attendance.

Children's shows tend to draw well, especially when there is entertainment for the children. In fact, one store found that they draw too well. When sponsoring DuPont's "The Wizard of Oz" locally, the store distributed twice as many tickets as there were seats. When a full complement of mothers and children turned up, a near-riot ensued. It was impossible to schedule a second performance because of union rules. Be as cautious in giving out tickets for a children's show as for a bridal show. If it is a show that is likely to draw a crowd, limit overage to 10% to 15% over the seating capacity.

Tickets Can Provide a Mailing List

Tickets for a fashion show may be used as a means of compiling valuable mailing lists for future shows or uses. A bridal show can provide the names of prospects for bridal services. Just include spaces on the tickets to fill in name, address, telephone number, and date of wedding, if set.

An excellent teen or business girl mailing list may be compiled in the same way. For teens, ask for school, class, and age, in addition to name and address. For business girls, ask for company name and address as well as their own.

Tickets for Door Prizes

The same tickets may be used for drawing door prizes. This saves the expense of buying numbered rolls of tickets and also eliminates handing these out as guests arrive. Just leave a space for name and address on the ticket.

USHERS DO HELP

If it is an open show or one to which tickets are given free, guests sit where they please. However, when a room is half or three-quarters filled, it becomes difficult to see empty seats and to find seats for several persons together. Ushers or hostesses to help guests locate the empty seats should be on hand.

If tickets are paid for and a capacity audience is expected, it may be wise to assign seats or tables. This assures that there is a place for each person and that he or she can find it. Of course, there will be complaints about where some seats are located and one or two may ask for a refund (give it to them!).

When the show is in a theater or auditorium that regularly employs ushers, it is a good idea to use these employees. They are experienced at seating people and also are thoroughly familiar with the particular room.

Incidentally, a theater can usually provide the tickets for you if you wish to assign seats. As you know, these must be properly numbered to tally with the seats in the house.

INFORM ALL PERTINENT PERSONS ABOUT THE SHOW

No matter who is producing a fashion show, there will be telephone and personal inquiries about it the minute the invitations are issued or publicity is released. For this reason, telephone operators need to know the answers or to whom the callers should be referred. In a store, salespeople in the departments involved also need this information. All of these employees can answer questions about time, place, and how to obtain tickets.

If a store is sponsoring the show, participating in a big group show, or providing informal modeling, salespeople need to know exactly which pieces are in the show in order to answer customer inquiries. A list posted near the wrapping desk or at some other accessible spot will suffice. There is nothing more infuriating to a customer than to try to buy merchandise that no one knows about.

Some stores that place special importance in having well-trained and informed sales personnel stage dress rehearsals of shows for them. This, of course, is ideal. It not only informs the salesperson completely, but it also provides excellent employee relations in making them feel a part of the production.

THE SHOW PROGRAM

Programs have a very real place in the planning of a fashion show.

Almost every big trade show or benefit plans a program to give the merchandise and its providers additional publicity. These programs may also include paid advertising to bring revenue. Trade shows need this to help underwrite expenses, while benefits raise extra funds.

Manufacturers and couturiers do not use programs (unless it is a special show of some type) because their presentations are for the purpose of giving potential buyers a preview of the whole collection. Afterward, the buyers or customers work with a salesperson in looking at the clothes and placing orders.

Occasionally, a fashion manufacturer gives a party to introduce a line to the press and special buyers. In this event, there is usually an attractive program.

A program is an appreciated detail for a retail store show. Customers love to be given something, even if it's only a program. It helps the store sell the merchandise because it makes it easy for the customers to check off what they like and to find it in the store.

Plan Ahead

While a program is, of necessity, frequently a last-minute thing, all information except the lineup of the clothes can be planned and prepared ahead of time. If art is involved in a cover, this may be completed and even printed early if the lineup is planned for the inside or separate sheets.

A detail that is too often overlooked is correct spelling of all names and trade names on the program. It is inexcusable carelessness to misspell any names.

The lineup of the clothes may be typed for the program as soon as it is completed in order to save time at the last minute. Corrections can be made as changes in the lineup are made. Just before it is released to the printer, make a final check for total accuracy.

Information to be Programmed

Information in the program may be arranged in any convenient and easily read way. The name of the show goes on the cover or top of the program. It is a good idea, for future reference, to include the date. Since the audience will want to know who the commentator is, it is convenient to list this name and those of any special entertainers before the lineup is given. Then follow with the fashions to be shown in numerical order, heading each group with its fashion theme. Make the descriptions as short as possible, but include color and fabric information. If designers' names and prices are to be given, include these with the description. A typical program might start like this:

"FASHION TAKES A TRIP"
Regent House Ballroom
Tuesday, June 9, 1970

COMMENTATORS: Jane Simmons and Ron Phelps, stars of the
Tomorrow Show, Station ABCD

Music by The Rovers

SCENE I.   TAKE OFF IN KNITS
1. Navy wool knit three-piece suit $98.00
2. Navy/white striped polyester shirt dress $70.00
(Continue in this form.)

If models' names are used for any reason (celebrities, society women, or teens), their names may precede the descriptions:

1. Mrs. John Jensen — Navy wool knit three-piece suit $98.00

Another alternative is to list the models at the beginning or end of the program in alphabetical order:

"𝔓ortraits of a 𝔖pring 𝔅ride"

an exciting showing of

𝔖ibley's 𝔅ridal 𝔉ashions

saturday, february 4

in sibley's tower restaurant

sixth floor

𝔄dmit 𝔒ne   3:45 p. m.

Ticket and program produced by Sibley's of Rochester, New York, for a semi-annual bridal fashion show reflect a feminine feeling.

*S*IBLEY'S

presents

portraits

of a

spring

bride

MARCH 1, MCMLXVII

The king of beasts lends a masculine touch to the program of a men's fashion show, "Sir Bates," presented for the press and buyers by Bates Fabrics. The fashion director of *Playboy* Magazine commentated.

MODELS: Susan Albert, Betty Conway, Sharon Ferguson, Bette Gates (and so on).

It is a customer service to note after each piece, or at the end if all clothes are from one department, where the clothes may be found in the store:

1. Navy wool three-piece knit suit $98.00
   Travelogue Boutique, third floor
                                    or
   All fashions from the junior departments on the fourth floor.

Credits for accessories, props, flowers, and the like are best given at the end under a heading:

Thank You Credits

Jewelry	(name of company)
Shoes	'' '' ''
Luggage	'' '' ''

(and so on for all credits to be given)

FAVORS AND GIVEAWAYS

It is strange but true that any audience, no matter how sophisticated, loves a free favor or gift. Any little giveaway adds to the pleasure and excitement of a show. Cosmetic and fragrance companies are most likely to be able to supply samples such as tiny vials of perfume or lipstick samples. The cosmetic buyer in a store may be able to obtain these from some of her key suppliers for a store show. It is difficult for an individual or organization to obtain samples because these companies are deluged with requests.

Charity benefits attended by a wealthy audience are often able to obtain fairly expensive favors, such as regular-sized bottles of cologne, full-sized lipsticks, scarfs, and similar items.

Arrange favors in an attractive way, such as in pretty baskets, and have them distributed by assistants at the show. Limit one to a guest.

Frequently excellent booklets and brochures are available from various types of companies. For a travel show, for example, airlines, tourist offices, resort hotels, and luggage manufacturers are possible companies to approach. All kinds of appropriate material are available from tablewares companies (china, silver, glassware) for a bridal show. For a holiday party fashion show, there are booklets on entertaining or recipes for parties.

Door Prizes

There is no doubt that substantial door prizes will help to build an audience. Most companies are deluged with requests from all directions to contribute door prizes for all kinds of events—from fashion shows to the Friday night bingo game.

Store buyers are often able to obtain merchandise from their biggest suppliers, but should use this privilege with discretion. A wardrobe of a certain specified value is a tremendous attraction to an audience, such as a new $300 spring wardrobe to be selected by the winner. Of course, this kind of prize has to be provided for in someone's budget—usually that of the department sponsoring the show or the sales promotion department. Trips that may sometimes be worked out with area airlines and hotels are exciting. Always arrange it for two persons—no one wants to go alone.

A major society charity show may be able to attract handsome prizes such as jewelry and furs from fine stores with wealthy clienteles. Some big events of this type have gone so far as to give away expensive cars. This type of prize must be provided for in the price of the tickets even though a local dealer may be willing to sell the car at a substantial discount.

Trade shows are able to obtain prizes from members or may possibly work out trips to interesting destinations with airlines.

Any company that contributes door prizes or favors does so for publicity. It is only fair that the sponsor of the show and the commentator make a special point of a blurb for the company and its product. Give printed credit in the program and runway credit by the commentator.

Gifting the Press

Shows given specifically for the press often provide substantial "goodies" and door prizes. Almost anything that is in good taste is acceptable. It may or may not relate to the show. Splits of champagne might be the favors for the opening of a collection or the launching of a new designer. At his "Pink Champagne" seasonal openings, Mr. John gives several of his hats as door prizes for the press.

GUARDING THE MERCHANDISE

The value of clothes and accessories for any fashion show runs into thousands of dollars. A couture or trade show can go well into a six-figure amount, especially if original samples are used. Thus substantial protection must be provided.

In a store the same staff usually produces all shows, and the same models are generally booked. These people know the rooms that are used and are aware of where and how thefts may occur. Thus they are on guard. However, it is sensible to take the extra precaution of having a female store detective in the dressing room. If male models are employed, station a male protection agent in their room. It isn't that the models are likely to steal, although this can happen, but that so many persons are involved that unfortunate losses can occur. Also, the merchandise should be watched while it is in transit to and from the show location.

A couture house or manufacturer's showroom is an intimate place, so care in handling and locking up merchandise generally suffices.

Any show in a public place, such as a hotel, club, or auditorium, demands guards from the minute the show arrives until it leaves. It is economical to employ persons from a professional protection agency (listed under "Guard and Patrol Service" in the yellow pages of the phone book) and give them specific instructions in writing as to how many agents are needed (male or female), where they are to be stationed, any special merchandise to watch, and the hours they are to be on duty. If merchandise is left overnight, it should be guarded or double-locked.

When expensive pieces are included, such as furs, fine jewelry, or couture gowns, book special guards to concentrate on these.

INSURANCE COVERAGE

Since types of insurance policies vary, it is impossible to specify here which kind of insurance covers thefts and losses during a fashion show. It is up to the show manager to check with the store or company involved to see if there are floater policies that cover this eventuality or if a special policy is in order. Consideration should also be given to liability insurance to take care of any injuries suffered by anyone in connection with the show.

PUBLICITY FOR YOUR SHOW

The greatest show on earth will not attract an audience if nobody knows about it. This means that publicity is an essential part of the planning of any show right from the beginning in order to draw an audience of the desired size.

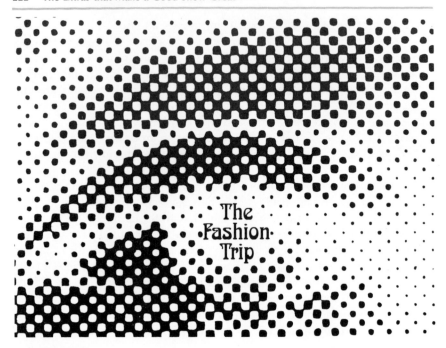

Invitation to "The Fashion Trip" show staged by *Seventeen* Magazine. Outside is in black and silver; (page 223) inside printing in terra cotta. Silver with black program cover coordinates (page 224).

Invitations Come First

An attractive invitation will interest the recipient instantly, pique curiosity, and make her (or him) want to come. Tie in the design of the invitation with the theme of the show and the type of audience (women, teens, men, brides, or whatever). An attractive, especially designed postcard is the least expensive to produce and mail. For a major show, such as a charity benefit, a handsome invitation in an envelope with an R.S.V.P. card for ordering tickets may be desired.

Be sure to give all essential information:

> type of show
> day and date
> time
> place
> ticket information
> how to obtain tickets
> price of tickets, if any

we promise you
a "showdelic" experience
when you take

The Fashion Trip

june 9, 1967
4:30 cocktails   5 o'clock show
waldorf-astoria   grand ballroom

R.S.V.P.

$15.00 (to be "transported")

Although social invitations are mailed about three weeks before an event, this is too early in the case of many fashion shows. Mail invitations to a store show ten days to two weeks beforehand so that it will be fresh in customers' minds. If mailed too early, they are likely to be misplaced and forgotten.

Invitations to a benefit show may be mailed very early — three to four weeks or even more before the event. The price of the tickets is usually substantial, so time is needed for a selling job to be done by the ticket committee. Also, the same group of people in any city tends to be invited over and over again to these benefits. Their calendars are booked

The Now Event—
SEVENTEEN's
mind-bending
Fashion Trip
into Fall
PROGRAMMED for June 9, 1967
Grand Ballroom
Waldorf-Astoria Hotel

weeks ahead, and they may pick and choose the events they prefer. So the earlier they receive your invitation, the better chance you have to sell tickets.

The press is another group of people whose calendars are always jammed. Their invitations should be mailed three to four weeks beforehand in order to assure attendance. They keep appointment calendars and will not forget. Trade shows that draw attendance from out of town send their invitations or announcements several months early because travel arrangements are involved.

Mail all invitations first class and hand stamped. Any other method is not in good taste and not safe from the delivery standpoint. It even pays to select the postage stamps to be used. For one gala show, a black memorial stamp was inappropriately used by the mailing house that handled the invitations.

Any invitations with a social connection, such as for benefits, are more attractive when they are hand addressed. The typewriter is acceptable for all others. Store Addressograph plates are generally used for invitation mailings.

Press invitations are often sent by telegram to assure attention. Be certain that complete information is given because editors and reporters have no time for detective work. Invitations have been received without a date or even without the name of the sponsor of the show. Busy recipients are likely to discard this kind of invitation.

Advertising

Most store shows are open to the general public, the purpose being to expose the merchandise to the largest possible number of potential customers, as well as to draw people into the store. For this reason, newspaper advertising becomes a part of the publicity plan.

Major advertising space is usually employed to publicize a major show such as a semiannual bridal show. One or two of these may be scheduled. For additional exposure, drop-ins may be used in the daily advertising. Other public shows may also use newspaper advertising.

Make the information about the show specific, including the kind of show so the reader will know whether the show is for her. It is wasteful to be careless on this point. Nothing is more disappointing than to draw the wrong customer—and the customer feels misled.

Windows

Store windows are an effective means of publicizing a show without any cost. If the windows are allocated to the department sponsoring the show, window card copy can also serve as an additional invitation to the crowds of people passing by. A tiny card in any other window does not detract from the display and is worth requesting.

Radio and Television

Short spots on radio and television are effective in building a show audience. Many stores sponsor local programs or buy time regularly. A

Best & Co.

cordially

invites you

to attend our

FALL-WINTER

BRIDAL SHOW

Tuesday, June 24th

at 6:00 PM

Bridal Salon

Third Floor

FIFTH AVENUE AT FIFTY FIRST STREET

(a)

A group of fashion show advertisements: (a) announcement of a bridal show, 2 columns, 8 in., Best & Co.; (b) Gimbels' 3-column full invitation to a bridal show; (c) a young fashion-show ad by B. Altman, 3 columns, 5 in.; (d) Alexander's full-page invitation to a young men's show.

GIMBELS NEW YORK AND ALL SUBURBAN STORES
OPEN TILL 10 P.M. THIS MONDAY AND TUESDAY . . .
OPEN TILL 6 P.M. WEDNESDAY.

GIMBELS

· Gimbels
cordially invites you
to be our guest at
"Wedding Impressions"
Spring-Summer
1970 Bridal Fashion Show

Stepping out of a Monet and into a new decade, the bride of
1970 emerges in all her radiance at Gimbels Spring-Summer Bridal
Fashion Show. Her gown: floating flowers and ribbons of grosgrain
on a misty scoop of organza by Christos for Galina. Rayon over
acetate taffeta_____ $260
Her headpiece: a fountain of nylon veiling, flowing to chapel
length from a floral embroidered helmet_____ $70
From the romantic collection of gowns for the bride and her attendants you'll see in "Wedding Impressions."

WEDNESDAY, JANUARY 7, 6:30 AND 8 P. M.
HOTEL STATLER HILTON GRAND BALLROOM

And at:
· Gimbels Valley Stream, Wednesday, January 14, 6:30 and 8 p.m.
· Gimbels Paramus, Monday, January 19, 7:30 p.m.
· Gimbels Westchester, Tuesday, January 20, 7:30 p.m.
· Gimbels Roosevelt Field, Wednesday, January 21, 7:30 p.m.

FOR TICKETS: Come to or call the Bridal Salon at the Gimbels presenting the show you wish to attend. For the New York show, call LO 4-3368
or pick up your tickets on the 4th floor in the Bridal Salon or the Jane Bell
Shopping Service. For other shows, phone the special Bridal Salon extension
for each store listed below. We hope you have a lovely time.

(b)

FASHION SHOW TOMORROW!

Come see our great new collection of
Young Colony® young fashions for Fall.
Commentary by the Broadway Star, Alan Howard.
See, hear and meet WMCA's Murray The K
and the Buchanans of "Medicine Man" fame. I p.m.

B Altman & Co

Sixth floor, Fifth Avenue store.
Summer Store Hours 10 to 5:30.

(c)

fashion show announcement may sometimes "hitchhike" onto a regular program. Of course, it is best to make the announcement at a time when the prospective audience is likely to be listening. An announcement about a business girls' show made during working hours would be wasted, while one made early in the morning while they are dressing might be most effective.

HOW TO OBTAIN EDITORIAL PUBLICITY

All editors, reporters, and commentators are looking for news. That's their business. A fashion show can be news for them if the story is pre-

THE NEW YORK TIMES, SUNDAY, MARCH 23, 1969

MEN'S SPRING COUTURE '69 STARRING VALENTINO FOR MEN, MR. FISH OF LONDON AND THE TOMORROW SHOP!

Now, in an unprecedented fashion show, Alexander's unwraps an exciting new world of dashing ideas for day and night wear. Effortless, unobtrusive, easy-going styling—by Valentino, by Mr. Fish, from our unique Tomorrow Shop. Come see this exclusive collection—a new kind of freedom in men's fashion! PUBLIC FASHION SHOWS: Monday, March 24th, 6 pm and 8 pm, Lexington Avenue store only. Narrated by Robert L. Green, Fashion Director, Playboy Magazine. Admission Free, Third Floor.

ALEXANDER'S

(d)

sented in a proper and timely way. This means that an outside person is helping you "sell" your show and is by implication suggesting attendance to the reader or listener. A nose for the kind of news these professionals are seeking can be cultivated by a little experience and by observing the kind of material they welcome. They cannot use non-news.

Newspapers

Women's page or fashion editors like to "scoop" the show, or tell about it beforehand, even if they write about it again after it is over. They also like "exclusives"—stories that are not given to other papers. In order to obtain preshow publicity, let the appropriate editor of your preferred newspaper know about the show approximately three weeks in advance so that she will hopefully save "space" to do a story the day before the show. Try to give her a newsy story "slant" (idea) and offer to take advance pictures or provide models if she prefers to use the paper's photographer. Don't badger her, but don't fail to follow up in an effort to get a commitment.

Carry through your promises to the letter. Take the pictures and have them in her hands on the promised date at the latest. Attach a caption to each picture so that it is correctly identified, with all names spelled correctly.

If the editor prefers to use her photographer, discuss with her how many models she needs, what type of clothes she prefers, and when and where the "shooting" (photography) will take place. If you carry out her wishes to the letter, she will not only thank you but will welcome future stories.

In either case, prepare a written "release" (story) to accompany the photos. This gives a "release date," or the time when the paper may "break" (print) the story. It includes a brief rundown about the show, starting off with the five "Ws" of writing a news story—who, what, where, when, why. Here is a sample opening sentence:

(who)   The Avenue Department Store will present
(what)   its annual travel fashion show "Fashion Takes A Trip"
(where)   in the Ballroom of Regent House
(when)   on Tuesday, June 9th,
(why)   to show a collection of clothes for summer vacations.

Continue with information about who will commentate, any celebrities or guest stars, models if there are special ones, and the major fashion themes. Either begin or end the release with the name of the contact who can provide additional information (see sample release).

FOR DEERING MILLIKEN

NEWS FROM

Dick Moore
and Associates, Inc.

For immediate release

DM

New York and
Washington, D.C.

Contact: Dick Moore/
Kay Degenhardt
265-0610

Night: UN 6-3005

THE MILLIKEN BREAKFAST SHOW STORY IN BRIEF

BIG BUYERS' SHOW RUNS THREE WEEKS AT WALDORF

The highlight of this ready-to-wear New York buying season opens on May 27

at the Waldorf-Astoria Hotel and runs through June 12. It's the sixteenth

annual Breakfast Show, sponsored by Deering Milliken, Inc., the textile

manufacturer. The original musical comedy, with an 8 a.m. curtain, stars

David Burns, Lou Jacobi and Phil Leeds, three of the funniest men on Broadway.

The audience--composed of more than 25,000 ready-to-wear buyers--will

be Milliken's guests for breakfast, then watch the hour-long musical comedy

that forecasts fall trends and shows women's fashions made by Milliken's

customers--manufacturers who make garments of Milliken fabrics and yarns.

# # #

200 West 57th Street, New York, New York 10019, Telephone 212-265-0610

Short press release announcing the Milliken Breakfast Show.

If you have enough news for more than one story, contact the second paper in the same way. Just remember never to give exactly the same story and pictures to two competitive newspapers. If you do, you won't get either one the next time.

Of course, all of the editors who have been contacted will receive invitations to come to the show. There is always a possibility that they will do a follow-up report.

Television

Almost every television station has at least one local women's program that uses events of interest to female viewers. Since these are frequently booked ahead for several weeks, contact the producer of the program and offer to bring models for a little fashion show. In many cases this can provide wide publicity, depending on the program and time of viewing.

Fashion shows on television require very special planning and handling (see Chapter 13).

Radio

Although television is the glamour medium of the air waves, radio can be very effective in disseminating news. There may be a women's program that uses local news like a fashion show. There is the possibility of obtaining interviews for a guest commentator during which mention of the show may be made once or twice.

In every city there is at least one disc jockey whom all the teens listen to and love. This kind of program generally welcomes news about teen events, such as a fashion show, to intersperse with the records. If a d.j. is invited to participate in the fashion show, he is all the more likely to contribute publicity by mentioning it during his program.

Contact the producer of any radio program just as you would for television. Of course, no visuals are involved, so any interview or publicity is easy to carry out.

Celebrity Interviews

Newspaper editors and television and radio broadcasters are always on the alert for celebrities or other persons of note who are visiting their cities. Anyone who comes to town to commentate a fashion show or to make a personal appearance can usually be booked for interviews which can, at the same time, publicize the show. The trick is to let the papers and stations know in time to plan or program appearances. A telephone call will suffice in most cases. A follow-up by letter may prevent misunderstandings or errors. Be sure to produce your celebrity at the appointed time and place.

Brian Aherne and Gertrude Lawrence being interviewed by Arlene Francis, center, to publicize the second "March of Dimes" fashion show in 1946. Courtesy of The National Foundation — March of Dimes.

Publicity Pictures

In providing publicity pictures to any medium, observe these ten essential rules:

1. Find a photographer who is experienced in taking publicity shots. He will understand exactly how the pictures must look and be prepared. Also, his fees will be less than a photographer who specializes in advertising or editorial photography. A portrait photographer is not appropriate for this type of work.

2. Book the photographer and models for one or two hours, depending on the number of pictures to be taken. Bulk your work into this time. It is costly, inefficient, and unprofessional to try to take one or two pictures at a time.

3. Plan your location (the scene of the shooting) wherever you wish, since publicity photographers are used to working anywhere. You do not have to go to their studio, although you may if you wish.

Cameramen focus for publicity pictures before the second "March of Dimes" fashion show as models prepare to pose for special pictures, 1946. Courtesy of The National Foundation—March of Dimes.

Publicity pictures posed against no-seam paper in a studio are very acceptable.

4. Take the pictures early enough to allow time for developing (publicity photographers are used to finishing in a few hours), writing and attaching captions, and delivering everything to the media.

5. Don't plan elaborate backgrounds because they do not reproduce well in newspapers or on camera. Pictures may be taken indoors or outdoors, but focus on the merchandise so that it emerges sharply and clearly.

6. Confine each photograph to one or two—or at most three—models because a group does not reproduce well.

7. Select outfits for publicity pictures that have news value. For this purpose, you can even use the most extreme pieces from the show. An editor does not want to publish a picture of something old.

8. For newspaper reproduction or television showing, select the sharpest, clearest pictures from among the proofs submitted. Anything blurred or soft is simply lost in reproduction. Pictures for newspapers are engraved in a series of tiny dots (look at one through a magnifying glass) called a "screen." Many papers use a coarse screen which loses a great deal of sharpness and detail from the original photograph. Anything out of focus is lost.

9. Prints supplied to newspapers must be glossy (they are called "glossies"). The usual size is 8 in. by 10 in. Prints submitted to television stations can be in the same size or larger, but with a special mat, or dull, finish.

10. Attach a caption to the picture by pasting it to the back and folding it over the front. Cellophane tape may also be used on the back for attaching. Never attach to the face of the picture. The purpose of the caption is to tell in two or three sentences what the picture represents and to give correctly spelled names, in order, of any persons who should be identified. If the pictures are exclusives for one medium only, type at the top of the caption, "Exclusive to . . . "

Sample Publicity Picture Caption

For release October 31, 1970

Exclusive to the *Daily Inquirer*

Doreen Dix of Channel 11 chats with Mrs. Thomas Sargent and Mrs. Lance Donaldson at a rehearsal of the Service Association's benefit fashion show to be held at the Carlton Hotel on November 1st. Miss Dix will commentate the showing of holiday clothes from the Avenue Shop. Mrs. Sargent will model the pink chiffon ball gown worn here, while Mrs. Donaldson will wear the pink lace.

CONTACT: Mrs. Schuyler van Palmer
                Service Association
                111 Park Avenue
                Saint Louis, Missouri
                Telephone No. 321-1234

Releases

For any show from which you expect to obtain publicity, press releases must be prepared and handed out. These are usually distributed at the door as the guests are leaving so that they can't rustle them dur-

FROM: ANN WALSH/DEL ROBERTS   PHOTO COURTESY HELENA RUBINSTEIN

FOR IMMEDIATE RELEASE   PHOTO EXCLUSIVE TO YOU IN YOUR CITY

HELENA RUBINSTEIN INTRODUCES "LIGHTWORKS" A TOTALLY NEW CONCEPT

IN MAKE-UP. Five exciting new cosmetics play with light in an

entirely new way: Lipshine, Eyeshine, Vinyliner, Lashbrow, and

Pat-A-Blush. Lips light up with "Lipshine" an ingenious "Splitstick"

half color, half pure gloss, and the colors are as cool as this

make-up news is hot: Lemonlight, a warm beige touched with lemon,

perfect as a toner to blend out a too-blue hue from the lips,

Firelight, a rosy peach with overtones of flame; Mauvelight, a

pink beige; Taupelight, an orange beige; Pinklight, a clear pink;

Coralight, a warm rust. Simply apply the color and with the twist

of the wrist apply the gloss from the same remarkable stick. All

the "Lightworks cosmetics debut in delightfully-designed black

and white polka-dot packages that make them accessories, not just

make-up.

                        -HR-

    r/xt

One of the publicity photographs with caption handed out at Helena Rubinstein's "Lightworks" show to introduce a new idea in makeup.

ing the show and don't have to hold them. These are on a nonexclusive basis.

Although reporters, editors, and broadcasters have seen the show personally, a release gives them accurately, in writing, a resume of the particulars and high points (see sample release).

Press Kits

A complete "press kit" of releases and pictures is appropriate on certain occasions, and is given to everyone at the show on a nonexclusive basis:

1. When there is news in the show in addition to the fashions themselves. One example is a show given to introduce a new fiber. In this case, various types of releases are included in the kit to provide the press with information on various aspects of the fiber such as a release on the development of the fiber, one on the company producing it, one on the scientist who developed the theory, one on the qualities of the fiber, one on the fabrics and uses for which the fiber is appropriate, and one on the fashions shown. Captioned pictures in the kit might include: the president of the fiber company; the scientist who conceived the fiber; the plant of the fiber company; and a selection of the fashions shown that exemplify the uses of the fiber—each with identifying caption attached.

2. When there is a show specifically for the press to release news to them. This might be a California swimsuit manufacturer who brings his new season's line to New York to show to newspaper, magazine, and trade press, and to television and radio commentators. Releases in the kit might be: a general release on the whole show; one on the entire line and its fashion message; and one on a special new construction in a swimsuit. Pictures with captions would represent the biggest news in the show. Only members of the trade press are likely to use the pictures because they work on small budgets. Other editors would use them for reference and make arrangements to take their own pictures for publication. They might bring a photographer to take action shots on the scene.

3. When the show is for a special purpose, such as the annual Neiman-Marcus Awards in Dallas, or a big trade show like the annual ski show in New York. In the case of the award show, biographical releases on all awardees and captioned photographs belong in the kit, as well as releases on the show itself. In the case of a trade show, releases would include: information on the scope of the whole show;

PRODUCT INFORMATION SERVICE

E. I. DU PONT DE NEMOURS & COMPANY

NEW YORK OFFICE • PUBLIC RELATIONS DEPARTMENT

350 FIFTH AVENUE, NEW YORK, NEW YORK 10001

DU PONT STAGES SPORTSWEAR
"SWITCH-IN" AT WEDNESDAY'S

A "Switch-In" musical fashion entertainment with a selling message for retailers on spring-summer switchery sportswear for '69 was presented by Du Pont's Sportswear Marketing Group, Thursday, October 31, at Wednesday's.

In the French sidewalk cafe atmosphere of Wednesday's unique little restaurant on East 86th Street an array of new pants, shirts, skirts and jackets in a variety of fabrics, all in Du Pont fibers, shared the spotlight with new display concepts for selling separates.

Prototype store fixtures, including a pipe-rack "jungle gym" on wheels, served as a moveable setting for the singing and dancing models and for the clothes.

The show included scenes on the pants look, the news in shirts, the peasant look in sportswear and "skin and bones" -- the new emphasis on the sheer see-through look. Slick shiny nylon jackets and pants, and the switchery concept of separates dressing -- meaning separates that go together without matching -- were highlighted in the last two scenes.

George McGuire, Sportswear Marketing Manager for Du Pont, introduced to the audience of retailers and fabric manufacturers, the guest commentator for the show, Edith Raymond Locke, Executive Fashion Editor of Mademoiselle Magazine. The show was produced by David Carter.

# # # #

Public Relations Contact: Kay Haverfield
Telephone: 971-4308 (Area Code 212)

PR-11 REV. 7-66

10/31/68

Press release given out by Du Pont at their "Switch-In" fashion show at Wednesday's in New York.

on the highlights from the fashion or equipment news standpoint; on any celebrities to make personal appearances, such as a noted ski champion; on social events during the show; and on the fashion presentation.

Packaging the Kit

Sometimes all of this material for the press is laid out on a table at the exit so that the press may pick up whichever releases and pictures are right for their purposes. At other times releases will be given out in a kit, while pictures (which are expensive) will be laid out for editors to choose. A third alternative is to put everything in a kit.

The easiest and quickest method for all concerned is to collate a complete kit of releases and pictures for every person who attends. This calls for the preparation of a kit or container to hold the material. The usual format is a cover with flaps inside so that the material will not slip out. It can be in an attractive color with printing and art on the outside. Folded size should accommodate $8\frac{1}{2}$ in. by 11 in. paper and 8 in. by 10 in. pictures.

Many companies or shows like to provide a special kit for the press as an additional favor. Some of these have been attaché cases, briefcases, clipboards, notebooks, and tote bags. You may be able to originate a container that would always be your signature. For years the Milliken Breakfast Show has handed out their kit to press and buyers alike in a zippered underarm brief case made of one of their plaid fabrics. Each year the plaid pattern is changed, but the case remains the same. There are so many of these in use that they have been spotted all over the world and are always a reminder of the name of the giver. The priest seen carrying one around Rome is still a puzzlement though!

ON SERVING REFRESHMENTS

Refreshments, or even a full meal, are a part of many fashion shows. Food adds to the ambience of the presentation and makes it more of an occasion. Almost everyone "wines and dines" the press, although sometimes they would prefer to get the story and leave.

These are some of the occasions when food is served at a fashion show:

Bridal Shows. Anyone producing a bridal show tries to make it as nice as possible. Tea, coffee, sandwiches, and cookies served from a tea table

Kit cover for press releases about Helena Rubinstein's "Lightworks" showing of cosmetics. Everything was carried out in black and white dots to match the packaging of the new products, including black limousines with white dots to pick up important guests.

are especially appropriate. A real wedding cake is a special fillip. Sometimes champagne is served.

Teen Shows. Teens love to eat, so they always enjoy something edible
at a show — or go to a show that provides something edible! Soft drinks
alone, or with potato chips and cookies, are sufficient.

Couture Openings. Paris couturiers and top American designers sometimes launch their new collections with a champagne opening.

Training Shows. If store personnel is asked to come in before opening
hours, a cart or buffet of coffee and rolls is appreciated.

Entertainment Shows. In these cases, the show may be incidental to a
luncheon or dinner, and not the main reason for the gathering.

Big Spectaculars. The Milliken Breakfast Show is an example of a big
show where the audience is served a complete breakfast early in the
morning. DuPont has given a number of black tie dinner shows, while
International Silk Association has given many beautiful dinner shows.

Press Shows. Any kind of feast may be set out for the press at any
time, from a champagne breakfast to a champagne buffet lunch, to a
champagne midnight supper. Just treat the press well.

ASSESSING RESULTS OF A SHOW

After every fashion show, a postmortem meeting of the show staff is
in order to discuss results and problems. At such a meeting, take careful
notes about any arrangements that should be changed and corrected the
next time. Type these later and file them properly for the future. In the
same way, make note of any suggestions for improving the show the
next time.

A record of how and where the tickets were distributed, how many
were given out, and the number that was actually used, is invaluable.

Also, copies of all publicity should be filed with these figures. If a
guaranteed number of guests was given to a hotel for purposes of serving food, jot down that number. A record of this information will save
time and possibly money when planning the next show.

Keep names, addresses, and telephone numbers of any suppliers who
performed especially well.

Another important check to make afterward is of the money spent in
relation to that budgeted. Any discrepancies should be checked and
noted for future reference.

13

The Specialized Fashion Show

There are certain types of specialized fashion shows that take place regularly and that have their own peculiar needs. No one should undertake a special type of show without knowing the specific requirements and the pitfalls, too. The major types of shows that call for additional know-how are discussed in this chapter.

TELEVISION

It is surprising that fashion is just beginning to come of age in television. Early attempts at TV fashion shows were criticized as not doing justice to the clothes. The growth of color broadcasting and the sale of color sets have given impetus to renewed interest in the medium as a stage for fashion. Also, people have become more and more visually oriented and are now responding to fashions shown on television.

Producing anything on television does not have the same elasticity of a runway or staged fashion show. In the first place, the clock is the master. Every segment of a program is timed, and commercials must go on as scheduled. A taped show may be cut and edited to fit the schedule, but a live show offers just one chance and must be perfect the first time. In the second place, action must always be within camera range and this may be a very small area.

Types of television fashion presentation that offer opportunities for publicity before audiences of thousands are discussed below.

The News Program

This is a short news note in a news program. The fashion story must be really newsworthy. If it has this attribute, be sure to approach the news department first, since they will not use it after someone else has.

The test of newsworthiness is: is it new . . . is it a trend . . . is it the first time. In all probability, a news spot of this type will be taped for inclusion in a news broadcast.

The News-Feature Program

This is a capsule fashion story handled in depth with a semi-news, semi-feature approach, and occupying a five or ten to twelve minute segment. This program delves into the background of the featured fashion idea. An example is the Millinery Institute's TV presentation of hats inspired by the movie "My Fair Lady." The program opened with a look at the millinery industry, moved on to the featured hat fashion show, and climaxed with some of the elaborate costumes and headgear from the movie production. This kind of feature is, of course, thoroughly planned and carefully produced.

The Millinery Institute, concerned with publicizing hats in connection with fashion apparel, was the first to take cameras to all the couture houses during Paris openings to develop another program of this type. Not only did they focus on the new fashions, but they went backstage for an intimate visit. This was so interesting and novel that it was accepted as a half-hour network special even though the Millinery Institute planned it for the purpose of promoting hats.

Feature Presentation with a Star

This approach involves obtaining a well-known star or celebrity to present or commentate on a group of fashions. It takes a "name" to pull a television audience. People will tune in to see a personality who, at the same time, gives authority to the clothes.

There are network shows whose hosts periodically present fashions, doing the commentary themselves. An example is Barbara Walters of NBC's "Today Show," who knows fashion well and handles the subject capably. Locally, a visiting editor of a national magazine or a designer who might be making a personal appearance can add this dimension. Stars of local women's programs also handle fashion material with authority.

The Sponsored Show

Any store or company that wants to present its fashion story in a commercial way on television may buy the time (reserve a specific amount of time and pay the required fee for it) and produce a show in any way it wishes. Cost of this time depends on the day of the week and the hour of the day or night, but is always expensive. "Prime time," when the largest audiences are viewing, is the most costly.

Production costs added to the time make an expensive package. For this reason, sponsored fashion shows are a rarity on television. When they do take place, it is almost always locally.

Because a fashion show needs action and variety, it is more satisfactory to tape the show beforehand than to produce it live. The TV camera for a taped show can roam wherever the producer wishes. For lower costs, the show may be taped in a studio. The advantage of taping rather than broadcasting live is the ability to cut and edit. Although this costs extra money, it permits a tighter, better, and more varied show.

Producing the Television Show

In putting a television fashion show together, two persons must work hand in hand as a team: the man who will get it on the air from the technical standpoint and the fashion authority who is responsible for the clothes and the fashion story. These must be professionals because TV has no place for amateurs. A flaw that may be covered up on a runway or may not even show at all is likely to be magnified on television.

These pointers will help to produce a professional television fashion show:

1. Go overboard on the number of models booked to assure a show with no gaps. Gaps are taboo on TV. Every split second is costly, and a lapse loses the fickle viewer very fast. Then add an extra model as a "spare wheel" because there is no margin for slow models. It is best to have a model for each outfit if it is a small show. If it runs more than eight outfits and the dressing room is immediately adjacent, the models will be able to change if they are professionals. Nonprofessional models cannot be expected to make a change this quickly. Remember to check whether nonunion or nonprofessional models can be used, and whether there is a scale of fees that must be paid. The types of models to select are discussed in Chapter 10.

2. Do not permit any "mugging" or cuteness on the part of the models. It is most unbecoming on this professional medium.

3. Block out camera movements in advance and rehearse, rehearse, rehearse. Nothing should ever come as a surprise to anyone working on the show. This is the road to disaster. Never permit a girl to appear out of sequence because it immediately throws off the commentator.

4. On television, the commentary is incidental to and complements the show. The best rule is to cut it short. It must never come across so strongly that it overrides the clothes. If the host of the show is to do

the commentary, complete written descriptions must be provided. It is also desirable for any other commentator, such as a visiting magazine editor, to have a written commentary or at least written notes. This makes a smoother presentation as it eliminates repetitive adjectives and insures that the commentator will not omit pertinent points.

5. Make any background sets simple so that they are a foil for the clothes. You are selling clothes — not wallpaper or furniture. Because the viewer's set is a small frame on which the human eye focuses, anything extraneous fights with the image you want to convey.

6. Although television broadcasts are largely in color, there are still black and white programs and sets. For this reason, thought must be given not only to how the colors will harmonize in color, but also how they will come through in black and white. If you are unfamiliar with how each color appears in black and white (for instance, red photographs dark), check the studio. Always avoid dead white because it reflects the lights (that's why male telecasters wear pale blue shirts that appear white on camera). Metallics are extremely difficult for a cameraman to handle, and white polka dots are guaranteed to drive him dotty.

BRIDAL SHOWS

One of the most important and certainly one of the most difficult shows is a bridal show. These are usually given by a retail store to publicize its bridal fashions and services. A growing trend is the citywide bridal fair staged by a local organization, such as a radio-television station, or by an outside company that arranges these promotions for profit. In this type of show, clothes may be provided by several different stores.

Bride's Magazine presents a beautiful show twice a year at a black-tie dinner in New York to present its new ideas in fashions and weddings for the coming season. Retail store buyers are invited to this Sunday-evening affair in April and October before the fall and spring bridal markets open.

As a rule, the big bridal shows for consumers are scheduled during the latter part of January or early February for the spring bride, and at the end of July or during August for the fall-winter bride. This is because the new fashions are available in the stores at those times and brides like to plan ahead for their big day.

When planning a bridal fashion show, follow these suggestions:

Appropriate foil for a *Bride's* Magazine fashion show is an all-silver curtain and series of doors through which models enter. Even the carpeting is in silver. Courtesy of *The Bride's Magazine.*

1. Make it the most beautiful show possible. Arrange every detail as if you were planning a real wedding. A wedding is a ceremonial occasion, so rules of etiquette must be followed. These can be found in any general etiquette book.

2. Include fashions for every member of the wedding party: bride, maid of honor, bridesmaids, and mother-of-the-bride. Because correct men's wedding clothes puzzle many brides—and certainly puzzle the men—show these too: groom and best man, ushers, and father-of-the-bride. Supplying an entire wedding party is sizable business and worth every effort put into the show. A wedding show is really a service to bridal customers. If men's clothes are not available in the store, a men's clothing store or a rental house may be willing to provide these in return for the publicity. Men's wedding clothes are often rented.

A rococo arch frames the opening on the stage for a bridal show at Higbee's of Cleveland. White fabric stretched over the runways not only looks appropriate but also protects the gowns.

3. It is awkward to try to mix fashions for the mother-of-the-bride with the bridal party clothes since she is not a member of the procession (the exception is some Jewish ceremonies). Make a separate sequence about a third or midway through the show for a selection of six to ten dresses. Bring each "mother" out separately. Send an usher along to accompany some, and a "father" with others.

4. Bridal lingerie, negligees, and sleepwear are often included in the show (see lingerie section in this chapter for how to model). Schedule this sequence about two thirds of the way through the show. Although it may be beautiful merchandise, it lacks drama in comparison with the other fashions in a bridal show. Therefore, it should never open or close the show, but should be tucked in where it will not detract.

5. Since bridal and bridesmaids' gowns are special, a simple stage setting is called for. It might be flowers and palms rented from a florist

(or borrowed in return for publicity). It might be several open picture frames constructed by the display department behind which models pose before going down the runway, or through which they step. It might be one big stained glass window constructed by the display department.

6. Show the clothes in complete wedding groupings: a bridesmaid or two, maid of honor, sometimes a flower girl or ring bearer, and the bride herself climaxing the grouping. Once in the show, use only children as attendants in European style. This method of modeling gives the audience helpful how-to information. To include men, as the bride comes on stage on the arm of her father, bring the groom and best man on at the end of the runway to wait for the bride. The groom can then accompany the bride off the runway, while the best man accompanies the maid of honor. The father may leave the runway alone first.

7. Give the show interest and variety by combining colors and accessorizing as imaginatively as possible. It's difficult to achieve variety in wedding dresses, and this is one way the look of the wedding

Filene's of Boston uses a ''Prince Charming'' story thread for a bridal show staged in a hotel ballroom.

Archways to frame the models and palms to lend color and texture make a setting compatible for a bridal show. Courtesy of *The Bride's* Magazine.

may be changed. Use imagination in headpieces and in the attendants' dresses. Shoes must be right—white or ivory for the bride and usually colored for the attendants (matching or contrasting). Most fashion offices keep a shoe wardrobe for this purpose. The quick shoe colorings are perfect for recoloring the shoes.

8. Flowers are essential accessories and can often be obtained from a local florist in return for the publicity. Try to find a creative one who can make up any special ideas or who may be able to suggest new ones.

9. Brides feel special and love special attention. Any little favor given them is appreciated. The boxes of cake mentioned in paragraph 10 are charming. A message inviting them to make the store their wedding headquarters and giving the name of the bridal consultant can be tucked inside. A shiny new penny pasted on a white card with a good luck message is another idea (prepare the cards near the time of the show because pennies tarnish). A fancy garter for each bride is appropriate as are samples of fragrance.

10. If possible, serve tea and coffee, or champagne, after the show. A bridal table, complete with cake, may be set up. If the store offers baking services, the cake can publicize that. If not, perhaps a local bakery will supply the cake in return for a credit in the program. An alternative to serving a cake is to give as favors a small piece of cake boxed and tied with ribbon like those given to guests at a wedding.

11. Models wearing bridal gowns do not pivot on a runway. They walk slowly enough for all to see, but not with the hesitation step used in a real wedding. Just a nice, happy walk.

12. Give special attention to hair styles. Be sure they are appropriate and that they all look well together. Give the same thought to make-up, especially that of the brides.

13. Petite models cannot be used for modeling wedding dresses because the dress with a train and veil overpowers them on a runway. To do justice to the merchandise, the model must be 5 ft. 7½ in. to 5 ft. 8 in. tall.

14. Remind models to smile and look happy. Modeling bridal clothes often makes them suddenly too solemn. They need to sparkle with animation. Lifeless models make lifeless shows.

15. Bridal shows demand more models than an ordinary show because the fragile dresses must be handled more carefully and require more time for changes. There are often many tiny buttons to undo. Using salespeople from the bridal department as dressers is wise because they are experienced in handling this merchandise.

16. Special attention must be paid all the way through to handling the perishable dresses. Cleanliness is essential in transporting, hanging, and wearing. If the dressing room floor is not carpeted, use sheets on the floor in the area where the "brides" are dressing. Tack them down or use wide masking tape around the edges.

17. Preferably, the runway for a bridal show is wider than the average 36 in. size. If possible, it should be at least 42 in. wide.

18. Bridal models should not be expected to go up and down any stairs when going to and from the dressing room, so avoid dressing rooms that are not on the same level with the stage or runway.

HIGH SCHOOL OR TEEN-AGE SHOWS

To satisfy the tremendous teen-age population and their love of clothes, fashion shows for girls are ubiquitous. Almost every retail store puts on a big back-to-school show in August or September, plus other seasonal shows throughout the year. There is a trend toward including some young men's fashions from a varsity shop in these shows, or even giving separate shows for boys.

Salient points for producing a lively young show are:

1. This is one show in which nonprofessional teen models are preferred because high school girls love to model and love to see their friends model; they can attract their friends to the show; they love to buy the clothes they model, and parents usually agree; they are more believable to a young audience; and they add an unprofessional charm to a young show.

2. High school models tend to be very subjective about the clothes they model. If they don't like it for themselves, they don't want to model it. To overcome this, explain that a model's responsibility is to show and sell the clothes to others who may like them. They usually accept this, since they all aspire to be models.

3. No matter how keenly the girls want to model, they are self-conscious and nervous. Instruction is essential, as is a thorough rehearsal.

The teen board of Higbee's, Cleveland, opens a rousing young show. Stage setting in the store's auditorium is limited to stark abstract shapes and steps that allow for movement.

Real teens model for a fashion show at Wolf & Dessauer of Fort Wayne, Indiana. The effective setting takes advantage of two of the audience's favorites—soft drinks and telephones.

4. It is best to give teen girls only one change or no changes if possible. They are unable to change as quickly as a pro. Thus, if there is a virtual mob of models, they can be dressed and lined up, and the show can proceed without a hitch. The only problem this presents is the noise and number in the dressing room, but this can be overcome with strict supervision. Also, for the reasons given in paragraph 1 above, the more models used, the better.

5. Teens love mail, so direct mail publicity is effective if an up-to-date mailing list is available. If not, don't waste the money. And don't waste money mailing to a general customer list.

6. Although teen-age boys may appear shy, they enjoy being dressed in new clothes and modeling with the girls. Just give them a chance to rehearse, and be specific in instructions.

7. Have a mimeographed instruction sheet to hand out to all teen models. Write down specifics about dates and hours of rehearsals and show. List any items they are responsible for bringing. Note the rules of the dressing room and rules for handling the merchandise.

8. Live music, or sound, is a requisite for a successful young show. A local popular group can usually be obtained at a fee that is not prohibitive. Ask the teen models who the group of the moment is. The right group can draw crowds, while the wrong one can keep them away. Failing live music, buy tapes of appropriate music, or make your own. A record player is generally unsatisfactory.

9. If there is commentary, a young person with whom the audience can identify is preferable to an older person. A popular disc jockey is good if he is given the essential information. Usually, a d.j. is better as a co-commentator. Teens don't need much talk. They want to look and judge for themselves. Here, more than anywhere else, informative commentary is preferable. Tell them why and how.

10. Since teens are always hungry, provide at least a bottle of soft drink. Local distributors of the better-known drinks usually will cooperate for the publicity. The most exclusive stores bend to serve soft drinks to young customers.

COLLEGE SHOWS

Each year, at the end of July and during August, when college shops in stores across the country are open, there is a rash of fashion shows to present college merchandise. All of the points given above in connection with high school shows apply here. Strongest interest in a college show comes from the girl who has just finished high school and will be a freshman in college. Additional notes:

1. Best models are college girls. Many stores organize an advisory board of college girls during the term of the college shop. This board is a natural for modeling.

2. Since college students are likely to travel to distant places to attend school, commentary is helpful if it emphasizes the merchandise that is appropriate for different areas and campuses.

3. The fashion director of the college show is wise to consult with the college board or college models about acceptable fashions and accessories. This is one place where college customers differ from their younger sisters. High school girls want authority for fashion, while college girls want to be the authorities themselves.

4. Since a percentage of college girls attending a show will be leaving home, additional merchandise can be included in a show for additional sales. Some of the categories are sleepwear and loungewear, small appliances, small decorative items such as pillows, even towels. Although large suitcases are awkward and unattractive when they are carried by a model, good-looking totes and duffles, which young people adore, are handsome accessories.

CHILDREN'S SHOWS

Although mothers select and buy the clothes for their children, most children's shows are designed to appeal to the children themselves, and so they stress entertainment. Perhaps this is an incentive for the mother to come. At least it solves the problem of hiring a baby sitter.

For five years, in the mid-1960s, the DuPont Company packaged an enchanting children's show and traveled it to a number of stores, one in a city. Professional actors and entertainers, scenery, and the whole works were provided to stores as a background for their own children's fashions that were made of DuPont fibers. The store provided the clothes and the local models. The five shows especially directed to children were: "The Wizard of Oz," "Rumpelstiltskin," "The Emperor's New Clothes," "Aladdin and His Lamp," and "Rip Van Winkle."

Here are some tips that will help bring off a children's show with a minimum of tears:

1. Consider carefully whether to use professional or nonprofessional children as models.
2. Try to keep mothers out of the dressing room. Provide an adjacent room and some coffee to keep them calm and occupied, or reserve seats or a table so they may see the show.
3. Each child needs his own dresser because they should not be left alone. They may disappear, for one thing.
4. While tiny tots are adorable and guaranteed to charm any audience, it isn't wise to use children under four years old.
5. Station someone at the end of the runway to assist children down the steps and point them toward the dressing room.
6. Plan some entertainment during the show that will appeal to children of the age that will wear the clothes in the show. It might be a magician or a clown. Although animals are not ideal occupants of a dressing room, they have great appeal for children. Live puppies, kittens, bunnies carried in the arms or in a basket enchant children.

Poodles are the best dog to lead on a runway. A bird in a cage is a possibility. Over-sized stuffed animals are appealing. Children's playthings on stage, such as slides and teeter-totters, are effective props.

7. Book a few more models than you would for an adult show because children become upset if they are hurried in a dressing room. Also, they frequently become ill and can't come at the last minute.

8. Music for a children's show can be very simple—just a piano or an accordion.

9. Most children learn little songs and routines quickly, and enjoy it. Thus simple numbers can be staged that everyone will enjoy.

MEN'S SHOWS

Although men's shows may never reach the popularity of women's shows, at least the showing of men's fashions is increasing, whether in a separate presentation or along with women's clothes. The mechanics of such a show are not so different from those of a women's show.

Several trade associations in the menswear industry stage seasonal shows to illustrate to press and buyers the men's fashions for the coming season. The best of these in recent years have had a book and music score with leads being taken by actors from the Broadway theater, and clothes modeled by professionals.

Be aware of these points which are pertinent to men's shows:

1. Schedule the show at a time when the greatest number of men can come—obviously outside of working hours. A lunchtime showing at a club frequented by men is a good occasion. An early cocktail showing after work is the other possibility. It is unlikely that men would attend a fashion show on Saturday when they want to sleep, putter, or play golf.

2. Tailor the show to a man's interests. It might be a showing of sports clothes. Add a demonstration by a pro, or a personal appearance by a sports celebrity such as a baseball or football star. Some of the men's magazines, sportswear and sporting goods manufacturers have such stars under contract to make personal appearances. They make them available for trade and store shows, among others.

3. Just as men now have a place in and add interest to women's shows, girls in a men's show make it more interesting. Note how the men's magazines, such as *Esquire*, use female models who are appropriately

Three scenes from a boys' and young men's fashion show spotlighting "The Country Look." Setting is simple and masculine; girls and entertainment are a part of the show. Courtesy of The Boys' and Young Men's Apparel Manufacturers Association.

dressed in their fashion photographs. After all, the sexes do to a large extent dress for each other.

4. Except for teen-age boys, professional male models are preferable. A nonprofessional is self-conscious on the runway, or may even balk at the last minute as one of the prominent men did at Elizabeth Hawes's famous men's showing in 1937, even though she warmed them with champagne beforehand. Select the most masculine types. In fact, they need not even be good-looking as long as they have the physique to wear clothes well.

5. If there are both males and females in the show, remember to provide two dressing rooms, as well as male and female dressers and guards, and all essential facilities for both rooms.

SWIMSUITS

Occasionally an entire beachwear show is given. In late spring and early summer, as well as at resort time, swimsuit segments snap up many a show. Swimsuit manufacturers show their lines to buyers and editors annually at showings on both the West Coast and the East Coast. These take place in August and September for the next resort and summer seasons. A few cautions assure the right look:

1. Select models carefully for the best effect on the runway. Qualities to look for in a swimsuit model are described in Chapter 10.

2. During fittings, check suits to be sure there is no transparency. If so, garments must be specially lined or worn over another garment. Provide tiny briefs or the postage-stamp size panty-girdles for all models for sanitary reasons as well as for a better look.

3. Many swimsuit models go barefoot and like it, but it is dangerous. There may be tiny bits of glass or other matter on floors that may injure someone. Use whatever sandals are in fashion that particular season.

UNDERGEAR AND SLEEPWEAR

So-called "intimate apparel" (an out-of-date name) is difficult not only to model, but also to make into an interesting show or segment in a show. The merchandise is often transparent or very revealing. Although attractive designs are available, since fashion has become a part of these classifications too, they do not have the excitement or impact of ready-to-wear on a runway.

(d)

To present Cardin fashions for men, Higbee's of Cleveland maintains a casual atmosphere at a showing in the Institute of Music. The male models show the menswear informally on four platforms spaced throughout the room while guests sip cocktails and the music group plays numbers from "Hair."

The majority of stores do not include intimate apparel in fashion shows except in the case of sleepwear which they may include in bridal, college, and teen shows. However, manufacturers must present their lines in an attractive and interesting way. In addition, there are occasional trade shows for this market.

A short nightgown being modeled at a showing in Warner's New York showroom. The attractive model is carefully put together from hairdo to hosiery for an attractive look on the runway. Courtesy of Warner's.

Some hints that may help when showing undergear and sleepwear:

1. For modeling girdles and bras, choose girls with great care, as explained in Chapter 10.
2. Because girdles and bras are so lightweight, a lining may be necessary. This should be checked during fittings in plenty of time to have

it done. A skin-colored nylon jersey works well as a lining. A rigid fabric cannot be used. However, pantyhose or tights under a girdle may be sufficient. Leotards are sometimes used under girdles and bras, but the color of the leotard must not give a grotesque or comic look. Light colors over a black or brightly colored leotard are not attractive. A nude color is best. Nude-color body stockings are excellent under some foundations.

3. A wisp of a cover-up does give girdles and bras a softness on the runway. Floaty, transparent sacques, either short or long depending on current fashion, may be made in different harmonizing colors for all models to wear.

4. Since girdles and bras, body stockings, and the like are foundations for ready-to-wear, the inclusion of some special fashion pieces gives substance to such a show. Warner's has effectively used a little revolving stage or platform to coordinate the two. Lights darken while a ready-to-wear fashion look is revolved into place. The model steps off the platform to model, returns, and is revolved out of sight while the companion models appear to show the right undergear for the fashion.

5. Transparent garments present the only major difficulty in showing sleepwear, such as in bridal sets. The solution is in adequate lining, or in the more modern approach of showing it over a nude body stocking.

HATS

Creating a good hat fashion show takes a bit of thinking. Models in early hat shows wore basic black dresses throughout the show, changing hats for each appearance on the runway. This, of course, makes instant changes possible, but it doesn't do justice to the hats. A hat is an accessory to an outfit and does not stand alone. It must relate to something.

The "Today Show" on NBC staged a most effective Easter hat fashion show. The stage setting resembled a huge Mondrian painting, squared off with blocks and bands of color. Some of the squares were open to reveal the head and shoulders of the models as the cameras spotted first one and then another. While the whole was not shown, the portrait shot gave the feeling of the total look. Each model showed three hats appropriate for her outfit. As a finale, the six girls came out to reveal their complete costumes.

The National Retail Merchants Association constructed a charming "Head Gear" boutique on stage as the device for showing young hats at

A hat boutique becomes the stage setting for a young headgear show at a convention of National Retail Merchants Association. Courtesy of Millinery Institute.

one of their conventions. Each young model dressed in a new fashion entered the boutique, selected a hat (preplanned), put it on, and walked down the runway.

Remember these suggestions for a hat fashion show:

1. Book models who look well in hats and who like to wear them. they do not necessarily have to have a pretty face, but an interesting one.
2. Let models know at the fitting how you want their hair done for the show. Hair must be compatible and complementary to the hats.
3. Never use a model with long hair unless it is a children's or teen-age show and the headgear goes with the young hair style. In fact, never use a model with an exaggerated coiffure of any kind.
4. Dress models from head to toe to present a total fashion look. If it is a trade or milliner's show, tie it in with ready-to-wear from a store or manufacturer. He can benefit as much as the hat designer.

SHOES

Shoes are more difficult to present in a fashion show than hats. Hats are at least elevated so that everyone can see them, while shoes can be seen well only by those with runway seats unless the runway is elevated to a very high height, which is unbecoming to the models and presents problems of undergear. Some device must be employed to bring out the shoes.

When Herbert and Beth Levine were given a Fashion Critics' Award for their shoe designs in 1967, they commissioned an exciting film to be made for showing at the presentations in the Metropolitan Museum, rather than trying to show shoes on stage. The newest techniques were used in the photography and effects which provided a much more dramatic presentation than a live showing ever could.

The semi-annual shoe fashion presentations to press and trade that the Association Fashion Service produces use live models for the total look, but slides for the detail of the shoes shown. This is probably the most effective way to do a shoe show.

Models select hats from the boutique to wear down the runway in the headgear show of National Retail Merchants Association. Courtesy of Millinery Institute.

Other means have been used, such as showing feet only, with bodies masked out by screens or panels. In one teen show, the girls wore painted barrels suspended from the shoulders by straps. These ideas defeat the purpose of a shoe fashion show, which is to relate new fashions in shoes to new fashions in clothes.

Here are several pointers to keep in mind when planning a shoe show:

1. Book models with medium-sized feet. It has been traditional in the shoe market for manufacturers to show their lines on a size 4B, which practically no female wears nor can relate to. Also, this small size is proportioned quite differently from an average size and thus gives a different effect. Sizes seven to eight are the average sizes sold, while model sizes range from about $6\frac{1}{2}$ A to $8\frac{1}{2}$ A.

2. Select the perfect stockings or socks to complement each pair of shoes for a total "leg look" and to coordinate with the ready-to-wear.

3. Present shoes as a part of the total look, with models well dressed in current fashions.

MATERNITY SHOWS

Yes, fashion showings of maternity clothes are given. Since several million babies are born each year, there is a potential audience and surely always will be.

The question is whether to use a regular model or to use an expectant mother. If luck is with you, there may be a good model who is pregnant at the time, but you can't expect an entire group of pregnant models. Magazines and newspapers frequently use someone who is pregnant to do their maternity fashion pictures.

It isn't practical for a maternity designer or manufacturer to try to show a collection or line on pregnant models. Furthermore, a nonpregnant fashion look is their criterion for maternity fashions. So when they are modeled, these lines are shown on regular models.

Since most lay persons lack the imagination to visualize how they would look in clothes, it makes sense to use pregnant models for a consumer show. Many women in the audience will be in their first pregnancy and uncertain about how to dress. Through word of mouth, women may be found to model. A store may obtain models through salespeople in the maternity department. Even a call to a well-known obstetrician isn't impossible. Of course, women in the last months of pregnancy should not be used.

Page Boy, one of the first companies to add fashion to maternity clothes, staged one big hotel fashion show in New York using all pregnant models. Florence Henderson, who was then pregnant, was commentator.

PATTERN AND FABRIC SHOWS

All of the pattern companies plan fashion shows of their patterns made up in current fashion fabrics, while many fabric producers do shows of their home sewing fabrics made into fashions with paper patterns. The fabric and pattern departments in retail stores do the same thing. Customers are particularly lacking in imagination when faced with putting a pattern and a fabric together to add up to a chic fashion. Because personal labor as well as money goes into such a garment, they are especially keen on seeing completed outfits for inspirational ideas.

A pattern-fabric show follows all of the rules and procedures for a regular fashion show. There are two particular advantages: A show may be entirely created from the standpoint of coordinating fabrics, colors, and silhouettes, as opposed to having to style a show from available ready-to-wear. The other advantage is that the clothes may be made for the models who will show them which saves time and money on alterations.

The one important precaution is to be sure the show is a real fashion show. Make selections in patterns and fabrics that transmit a fashion message, and line up the show to emphasize these, just as you would with ready-to-wear.

BEAUTY IN A FASHION SHOW

There was a time when beauty was thought to stand alone. Today's more sophisticated approach recognizes that the beauty look is a part of the fashion whole. Thus it becomes an integral part of every fashion show, whether as the unsung look the models present, or pointed up as a special feature.

Models must always reflect the current beauty look attuned to the type of clothes they are modeling—daytime, sports, cocktail, or evening. This encompasses not only makeup but also hair. It is the responsibility of the fashion authority on the show to tell the models what fashion look she wants represented, and even to provide the cosmetics if it is a new idea. The ideal situation is to have a cosmetics representative actually do the makeup on the models. Hair may be done by a hair-

Scene from a Yardley fashion show staged by Brandeis of Omaha, Nebraska. Models wear slickers to dramatize lip slickers. Courtesy of Yardley of London.

dresser, or a hairdresser may be stationed in the dressing room to comb the models' hair.

Makeup demonstrations on stage have been tried, but are actually boring because they are slow and the majority of the audience is unable to see the details. The best solution to a makeup segment in a show is the use of slides or film. Film is costly unless it is supplied by one of the major cosmetic houses, but slides may be made easily and inexpensively. Anyone who is at all handy with a camera can take color pictures which, in turn, may be developed into paper-mounted slides for a simple Carousel projector.

Models' hair styles may also be shown effectively in detail by a similar use of slides.

OUTDOOR SHOWS

At the proper time of year, outdoor shows are frequently given. It seems to be easy and simple, but sometimes the problems are even bigger than for an indoor show.

The biggest problem is the weather, which can never be counted on to behave even if it is checked out with local weather authorities and the "Farmer's Almanac." Alternate provisions must be made and the audience told what to do in case of rain. Usually an outdoor site, such as the parking lot of a shopping center, is used because there is no indoor spot large enough for the show. In this case, publicity and invitations may note, "In case of rain, the show will be held at the same time on the following day."

When going outside, everything must be transported to the scene — from chairs to amplification. If the show is at night, strong lighting must be available. Power lines for lights and amplification have to be run out. There must be dressing rooms close by, or at the scene. All of this presents a tremendous task of organization.

Be sure there are enough hands and facilities to stage an outdoor show, or plan something else. It can be fabulous if all goes well — or fatal if it doesn't.

A fashion show given by The Virginian-Pilot of Newport News, Virginia, at The Dome in Virginia Beach, uses screens above the models to link beauty to fashion.

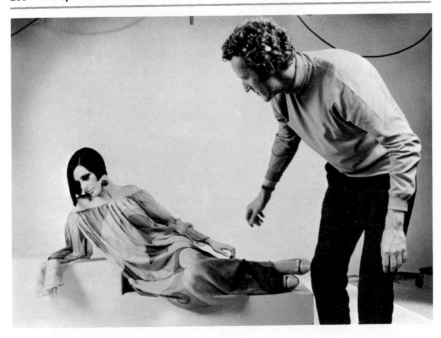

William Claxton directing model Ellen Harth during the filming of the fashion show "Basic Black." Courtesy of Claxton Productions.

THE FILMED FASHION SHOW

Aside from expense, a major problem of producing a fashion show on film is the time involved. Six months is not too long to allow for the whole project, and three months is a minimum. This means that clothes may have to be especially designed for the production in order that they will still look new and timely by the release date.

The filmed show has advantages as well as disadvantages. The cameras and models have the whole world available for settings and excitement, limited only by budget. New techniques in movie making may be employed to add even more interest. Editing can eliminate any segments that turn out to be less interesting. There can be retakes where a scene just doesn't come off or where something doesn't look right.

The biggest disadvantage, aside from expense and time, is that a model in a film is more remote than a model on a runway. Thus the audience cannot identify as easily with the clothes shown in a film. It presents a glamorous dream world, rather than a world that is there and possible for her.

Nevertheless, the fashion show on film might well be the next big development in fashion-show business. In fact, film may be the medium that will really make the fashion show a fine art.

Bibliography

Brockman, Helen L., *The Theory of Fashion Design,* New York: Wiley, 1965.

Chase, Edna Woolman, and Chase, Ilka, *Always in Vogue,* New York: Doubleday, 1954.

Carson, Ruth, "Your First Look," *Collier's,* October 17, 1936.

Crawford, M. D. C., *The Ways of Fashion,* New York: Fairchild, 1948.

Drygoodsman and Southwestern Merchant, Issues of February 10, 17, 24, and March 10, 1917.

Fashion Group, Inc., The, *Bulletins,* 1932–1968.

Fortune, "The Dressmakers of France," August 1932.

Hawes, Elizabeth, *Fashion Is Spinach,* New York: Random House, 1938.

Hurlock, Elizabeth B., "Fashion Dolls and Their History," *The Antiquarian,* December 1929.

Jones, Candy, *Make Your Name in Modeling and Television,* New York: Harper, 1960.

Langlade, Emile, *Rose Bertin,* New York: Scribner, 1913.

Levin, Phyllis Lee, *The Wheels of Fashion,* New York: Doubleday, 1964.

Morton, Grace Margaret, *The Arts of Costume and Personal Appearance,* New York: Wiley, 1964.

New York Times, The, Issues of October 4, 6, 7, 1942; October 30, 31, November 3, 1946; August 27, 1948.

Pickens, Mary Brooks, and Miller, Dora Loues, *Dressmakers of France,* New York: Harper, 1956.

Poiret, Paul, *King of Fashion,* Philadelphia: Lippincott, 1931.

Powers, John Robert, *The Powers Girls,* New York: Dutton, 1941.

Quant, Mary, *Quant by Quant,* New York: Putnam, 1966.

Saunders, Edith, *The Age of Worth,* London and New York: Longmans, Green, 1954.

Scheinfeld, Amram, "Broker in Beauts," *Esquire,* January 1936.

Stevenson, Margaretta, *How the Fashion World Works,* New York: Harper, 1938.

Vogue, Issues of March 5, 12, 26, 1896; November 1, December 1, 1914.

Warburton, Gertrude, and Maxwell, Jane, *Fashion for a Living,* New York: McGraw-Hill, 1939.

Wilson, Jane, "Fashion at the Box Office?," *Status & Diplomat,* April 1967.

Women's Wear Daily, Issues of August 15, 17, 18, 1914.

Worth, Jean Philippe (translated by Ruth Scott Miller), *A Century of Fashion,* Boston: Little, Brown, 1928.

Index

33955
C.1

Corinth

Fashion showmanship

DATE DUE

OCT 28 70		
NOV 7 70		
OCT 2 2 72		
JAN 2 9 1974		
FEB 27 75		
MAR 31 75	DISCARDED	
MAY 9 75		
MAY 3 0 1975		
May 28 77		
OCT 91		
OCT 91		
NOV 91		
DEC		
8-22-95		
1/24/07		